KILL FEAR BEFORE FEAR KILLS YOU

JP VASWANI

wisdom tree

Disclaimer: While every precaution has been taken in the preparation of this book, the publisher and the author cannot be held responsible for errors or omissions, or for any damage caused by the use of information contained therein as it does not constitute medical advice and should not be construed as such.

ISBN 978-81-8328-451-6

Published by
Wisdom Tree
4779/23, Ansari Road
Darya Ganj, New Delhi-110 002
Ph.: 23247966/67/68
wisdomtreebooks@gmail.com

Printed in India

Contents

PART I

How Fear Kills Us

1

We are All Victims of Fear

The famous essayist, Montaigne, once confessed: 'The thing I fear most is fear.'

Fear casts its dark shadow over our lives at one time or another. We are prone to fear almost instinctively. Neither the biggest nor the smallest of us is exempt from fear. The most powerful nations fear their rivals and neighbours. Politicians are afraid of losing elections. Students are afraid of failing in examinations. Mothers are afraid about their children's safety...the list is endless.

Fear is the one mark that characterises us children of a sceptical age. We are afraid of the future, afraid of poverty, of unemployment, of dishonour and disgrace, disease and death—it seems to me that sometimes, we are afraid of life itself!

We live in constant fear of losing whatever little we have. I remember a lady—she had a little metal box with some gold jewellery in it. She was our guest for some time, when I was a little boy. We noticed that she was constantly worried about the little box. She spent sleepless nights, often getting up to check if her gold was intact. She was terrified that someone would pilfer it. It may have been her most precious possession, but it gave her no joy!

We live in fear; we work in fear; we walk in fear; we talk in fear. We move through life from one fear to another, feeling crushed beneath the weight of a woeful existence.

Fear is at the root of all our problems. Fear is the starting point for all evil. Fear gives rise to most of our misfortunes. Living in constant fear saps our vital energies, leaving us too drained and exhausted to savour the joy of life. Fear paralyses the mind, just as a stroke paralyses the body. It strikes at the nervous system; it causes stress and tension. It undermines our well-being. Worst of all, it robs us of happiness and destroys our peace of mind.

It was Marie Curie, the iconic scientist, who said: 'Nothing in life is to be feared; it is only to be understood.'

Alas, many of our fears are imaginary! Take the case of a student. He has worked hard, prepared thoroughly for the examinations. But when he enters the examination hall, he is gripped by fear. He breaks out in a cold sweat, his hands tremble, he thinks that he has forgotten everything, he is convinced he is going to fail…

This is imaginary fear at its worst. And imaginary fear afflicts multitudes of people. The great writer, GK Chesterton, said: 'If I had only one sermon to preach, it would be a sermon against fear.'

A distinguished psychologist describes fear as 'the most disintegrating factor' in human personality. Anxiety and worry are closely allied with fear. Dr Smiley Blanton, a famous psychiatrist, declared: 'Anxiety is the great modern plague. Thousands upon thousands of people either destroy their lives or frustrate them, all because of their preoccupation with anxiety, worry and fear.'

There are people who live continually in fear, without even being aware of it. I know there are people who have forgotten what it is to be happy and relaxed.

A young woman once said to me, 'When I got up this morning, I felt so peaceful and content. Then suddenly, this dreadful feeling came upon me that I should not be feeling so relaxed...that there were so many things to worry about!'

There are many people like her who live in a permanent state of anxiety. They will not be able to specify what they are afraid of. They just suffer from persistent apprehension about something or the other. They are afraid that something terrible will befall them sooner or later—though they will never be able to tell you what it is!

Imaginary fear, the fear of the nameless, causes havoc in people's lives. Some time ago, a rumour spread like wildfire across the United States that a white powdery substance capable of causing anthrax was being secretly dispersed all over the country. The fear psychosis that this rumour generated was tremendous. People became distrustful of all white substances, including talcum powder, common salt and castor sugar!

In 2004, the tsunami that struck South Asia affected hundreds of people. Thousands of fishermen, who had been affected by it, are afraid of going out into the sea. They do not want to take the risk of carrying on with the only job that they know...because they are afraid that the tsunami may strike again.

I often narrate the story of the businessman who refused to fly because his father was killed in a plane crash. I asked him how his mother had died. 'She died peacefully, in her sleep,' he replied. That had not stopped him from going to bed every day!

Many people live in constant fear of ill health. They are constantly afraid of catching some deadly disease. In fact, many of us are constantly plagued by myriad fears concerning our health.

Unfortunately, there is an information overload about diseases. Perhaps this is not bad in itself for it keeps people aware, alert and health-conscious. But it has had the unhappy effect of making everything 'risky' or 'unhealthy' or 'poisonous'. Some people tell you not to eat potatoes; others tell you not to drink milk; some say that all oils and fats are bad; others tell you not to add salt to your food...and you live in constant fear of a heart attack, or cancer, or a hundred diseases that may strike you in the middle of the night.

People go to doctors with various complaints. The doctors carry out certain tests to rule out the presence of any risky factors. When these tests reveal nothing to worry about, they assure their patients that they are fine. But these people are still not satisfied. It is as if they are disheartened that their tests are negative. They may even decide to go to other doctors who, they hope, will diagnose that something is wrong with them!

Alas, this fear neurosis is aggravated by books, magazines and internet information on 'danger signals' which we are asked to watch out for. Symptoms are listed and we recognise them to be ours and off we rush in search of another doctor.

Why is it that a vast majority of us live perpetually in fear of something or the other? Perhaps one reason is that we are lonely. The deepest tragedy of modern man is his loneliness. In spite of an ever increasing number of clubs, hotels, restaurants, parks, museums and theatres, people feel lonely and lost. A distinguished visitor to the US was taken to a cinema. He saw hundreds of people standing in queues to obtain a ticket. The visitor remarked, 'The Americans must be very lonely at heart; else, there would not be such endless queues at the cinema!'

Yes, if we were to confess the truth to ourselves we will not deny that we are lonely. We lack the security of protection. We are like a child, who, taken to a fair, lost his mother in the crowd. The child rent the air with cries of 'Ma! Ma!' Alas! We have forgotten even to cry out for our Divine Mother. We are like the orphan who was never tired of complaining that there was no one to care for him in this world.

It is this sense of loneliness that leads to a feeling of frustration and many of us begin to feel that life is not worth living. Not long ago, I heard of a millionaire who committed suicide, leaving just a brief note on his writing table: 'I feel lonely. Therefore, I have decided to kill myself.'

Life has become nothing but a burden to untold millions. It is true that only a few commit suicide. But the rest of us continue to live tense, joyless lives. Many people die premature deaths. Loneliness burdens the hearts of people, sapping their strength, eating into their vital energies. Little wonder then that heart diseases are on the increase. Hypertension is a common ailment, even among the young. Nervous breakdowns are taking a heavy toll. A cardiologist I know told me that more and more people below forty have been succumbing to heart attacks in recent years.

People feel lonely and lost, they feel abandoned, forsaken and forlorn. They have lost the sense of security which belongs to them as children of God; they have fallen into the abyss of fear.

Fear is a poison that quickly circulates through the entire system, paralysing the will, producing queer, unpleasant sensations in the mind and the heart, and sometimes causing unhealthy conditions like ulcer, acidity and fainting fits. Fear is a great foe of man. It must be uprooted before it overpowers you!

2

Fear Can Corrode You

Psychiatrists, pastors, counsellors and spiritual elders confirm that the general level of fear among people is on the increase today. It seems to extend across all walks of life and to all kinds of people. Children are beginning to dread school exams; smart young graduates develop cold feet before they face an interview; mothers worry non-stop about their offspring; young couples agonise over their savings and their budgets; old people are terrified of insecurity and loneliness; high-flying executives at the peak of their professional careers give in to stress and tension over fears of rivalry and competition.

Drop a little quantity of potassium permanganate into a large container of water. You will see the water turns pink almost instantly. Just the same way, fear spreads quickly through one's life and personality.

The United States of America is one of the most buoyant, high-spirited, optimistic nations of the world. The Americans love life, with all its challenges and rewards. They live life on the fast track. They work hard and they play hard too. But we saw how fear psychosis gripped this energetic nation after the terrible day we now call 9/11!

That was of course, an extraordinary event—the kind of event that does not happen every other day, praise be to God! But life is full of situations that seem to trigger off fear.

A middle-aged housewife went to her neighbourhood grocery store with her monthly shopping list. She greeted the shopkeeper cheerfully, for she had known him long.

'How's business these days?' she began.

The shopkeeper was filling up new tax forms which had become compulsory for all small businesses. He was confused, bewildered and slightly scared. What if they raided his shop? What if they insisted on checking his accounts? What if they decided to 'seal' his shop for irregularities which he was not aware of?

'How's business these days?' repeated the cheerful customer when she got no reply at first.

'What can I say, Madam,' he sighed, pushing aside the tax return forms. 'Life is tough. Prices are going up. Did you know *tur* dal costs forty rupees a kilo at wholesale rates? I don't know how I can continue in this business for long!'

The lady was dismayed—*tur* dal at forty rupees! And that too at wholesale prices! 'O my God,' she thought to herself, 'that means he will charge me at least forty-five rupees per kg!' Hastily, she began to make a few calculations. With three growing children to feed, she was very conscious of her monthly grocery budget and had to walk a tightrope between overspending and depriving her family of good food.

'What's the current price of *tur* dal?' she demanded suddenly.

'Oh, it's still at thirty-four rupees a kilo,' was the reply.

She took a quick decision. '*Bhaiya*, send me a fifty-kilo bag right away, and add it to my bill this month,' she said. She made up her mind that she would now buy in bulk and store for the months to come. Of course, she had not budgeted for this large quantity of dal. But she would cut back on something else, though she could not imagine what it would be.

When she returned home after placing the order, she was not the happy, relaxed woman who had walked to the shop just a few minutes ago. Inflation, rising food prices, her monthly budget, the children's school fees, the husband's promotion and increment—everything had jumbled up into a complex fear in her mind now. How was she going to manage?

People are anxious when the budget is presented in parliament. People worry when OPEC countries raise oil prices. People are afraid when foreigners come to live in their locality. People worry when share prices fall. Anything and everything triggers fear these days!

The logic of fear is truly illogical. We are afraid of losing our jobs, but we are also afraid to go out and seek new positions. I know some people who are terrified of contracting a major illness, but they are even more scared to meet a specialist and go through a series of tests. Some young women are afraid of marriage as they feel that they would lose their identity, but the idea of remaining single makes them feel insecure. There are very many old people who are terrified of the years that lie ahead of them and yet, they are haunted by the fear of death.

As I said, we are afraid to die, we are afraid to live because life has become so complicated, risky and insecure.

A ship in the harbour is safe, goes the saying, but that is not what ships are built for.

Absolute security and freedom from stress and anxiety are unreal conditions. I am very fond of the story narrated by Norman Vincent Peale, whose friend came to him with problems galore.

'I am fed up of my fears, my insecurities and my mounting tensions,' he said to Dr Peale. 'I want to move away from it all. I am going to sell my business. I shall get rid of my apartment here in the city and I want to move out to some place where I can have perfect peace and quiet!'

'Perfect peace and quiet…hmm…yes,' nodded Peale thoughtfully.

'You have travelled far and wide, Dr Peale,' said the man anxiously. 'Have you come across such a place as the one I seek? Can you recommend a suitable location for me?'

'I know one place that is not very far from here,' Dr Peale said to the man.

'Not very far from here—in New York?' exclaimed the man with incredulity. 'Is that possible?'

'Yes, right here in the heart of New York,' nodded Peale. 'I have known many people who have moved there over the years and they certainly don't have any complaints.'

'Take me to this place at once,' demanded the visitor. 'Please Dr Peale, I have got to see this place at once. I would like to move there as soon as possible!'

'Right, let's go,' said the wiser man. The men got their hats and coats and set off briskly.

Two blocks away from Peale's office, they turned into a shaded lane and Peale led him down the pavement till they faced massive, sturdy iron gates set between high walls.

'Here it is,' he said with a flourish, pointing to a cemetery that lay behind the closed gates.

'But, you can't be serious!' cried the visitor. 'You can't expect me to live in a graveyard!'

'My dear friend, this is the only place I know where there is the "perfect peace and quiet" that you demand. As I said, the dead have no complaints whatsoever. Would you like to move in with them?'

Dismayed, the man shook his head in dissent.

'In that case, you must learn to face life more confidently and positively,' said Dr Peale, beginning to walk away from the abode of perfect peace and quiet.

The man followed him hastily. He certainly would not demand absolute peace and quiet anymore!

Yes, absolute peace, absolute security and safety are not conditions of life and living.

3

Life Takes Courage

Whenever I am travelling abroad, people ask me why we do not observe Mother's Day in India at the same scale as they do. My reply to them is, 'Every day is Mothers' Day in India!' Indeed, where would we be without our mothers?

Mothers are our unsung heroines. Every day, day after day, they bravely take on the task of feeding, clothing and taking care of their children and families. They walk them to school, help them with their homework. They wash and iron, cook and clean. They balance budgets, they plan for the future. They participate in community activities, observe festivals, fasts and holy days. Their work never stops. Yet how many of us appreciate their courage?

Courage is the key! To live a full life, to live according to God's plan, to live life purposefully and meaningfully, requires courage.

Life demands of us that we live with courage. Winston Churchill considered courage to be the greatest of all virtues because we cannot exhibit any other virtue without it. Without the courage to act, justice would be impossible. Without the courage to love, compassion and understanding would not exist. Without the courage to endure, faith and hope would not flourish.

Linguistic experts relate the English word 'courage' to the French word '*coeur*', which is the French word for 'heart'. Courage is born of the heart. It is the heart's response to the impulse of fear.

Tagore's immortal hymn begins with the words: *Where the mind is without fear…*

Where the mind is without fear…that is where the land of freedom lies. For fear and freedom cancel out each other. If you are afraid, you cannot be free. And courage can liberate you from the clutches of fear.

For those of us who live by our faith, as well as those who place their belief on science, life poses a series of unanswered—at times unanswerable—questions. Why do bad things happen to good people? Why did a young, intelligent man, husband, father, brother and son to a family of wonderful people have to die of a rare, unheard form of cancer? Why are beautiful young babies sometimes born blind or deformed or spastic? Why are the nations of this world piling up a nuclear arsenal that can destroy the planet ten times over?

Truly, as someone once said, to be sentenced to life is to be sentenced to death! And that is why, cowards die several deaths.

Life is full of uncertainties, the unknown and the unknowable. Experts recommend that we develop what they call 'a high tolerance for uncertainty' if we are to live in peace, even while being aware that so much in our lives is outside our control. Losing control, living with uncertainty generates fear and this fear can be conquered by the right attitude—love, kindness, faith and compassion.

The Bhagavad Gita tells us:

Meet the transient world
With neither grasping nor fear,
Trust the unfolding of life
And you will attain true serenity.

The uncertainties of life have to be taken on, in the spirit of acceptance. Escape and running away are no solutions.

It was Helen Keller who said:

> Security is mostly a superstition. It does not exist in nature, nor do children as a whole experience it. Avoiding danger is not safer in the long run than outright exposure. Life is either a daring adventure or nothing.

Attitude Counts!

The First World War was described as 'the war to end all wars'. Sadly, just a few decades afterwards, the Second World War was fought, killing thousands more. And now, people shudder to mention another war, which, they feel, may destroy planet earth altogether.

In 1950, the Chinese Communists invaded Tibet and within a year, the Tibetan spiritual leader, the Dalai Lama, had to take over the reins of government, when he was barely sixteen-years old. In 1959, after a difficult and trying period in which Tibetan culture and freedom were systematically being eroded, he was forced to escape from Lhasa under the cover of night. Exiled to India, he and his followers faced tough challenges, not only to acclimatise themselves to a new country, but also to protect and rebuild their cultural and religious institutions. The Dalai Lama says that it was his spiritual practice that gave him the courage to look for solutions to their many problems. 'The perspectives of compassion, calm and insight,' he writes, 'are essential to daily life and must be cultivated in daily practice.'

The terrible forces of terrorism, strife and divisive politics are rearing their ugly head all over the world, ushering in wave after wave of violence. Often, people find themselves caught up helplessly in conflicts that unsettle them—conflicts in which they are not even involved, but which sweep across their lives nevertheless. Pain, anger and fear take hold of their hearts. This is what happens in several families, communities and nations.

Similar conflicts and tragedies, on a far worse scale, swept over Cambodia, Bosnia, Rwanda and Kosovo. Again and again, the victims demonstrated tolerance, understanding and courage—courage to forgive the unforgivable and to release their hearts from the clutches of fear and hatred.

Victor Frankel was a survivor of a Nazi concentration camp. Here is what he says in his memoirs:

> We who lived in the concentration camps can remember those who walked through the huts comforting others, giving away their last piece of bread.... They may have been few in number, but they offer sufficient proof that everything can be taken from us but the last of human freedoms...the freedom to choose our spirit in any circumstance.

A wise thinker once pointed out that there are two great sources of power, two great forces of strength in this world—one of them is vested in those who are not afraid to kill, hurt, wound, maim and destroy while the other is vested in those who are not afraid to love, forgive, heal and be reconciled.

We must be unafraid to love, for love requires courage. I have always believed that the power of love is far greater than the power of hatred. If we are to confront the dark forces of destruction and annihilation, we must use the greatest weapon in our possession—the power of love.

Love is not weak. Love is not sentimental. And love is not always easy!

Once, Mother Teresa was being interviewed for BBC Television. The interviewer remarked that in a way, the life of service might be much easier for her than for ordinary householders. After all, he pointed out, she had no possessions, no insurance, no car and no husband to care for!

Mother Teresa smiled and said to him, 'I'm married too!' She held up the ring that nuns of the Order of the Sisters of Charity wear, to symbolise their 'marriage' to Christ. She added, 'He can be very difficult at times!'

It takes courage to love!

Equally, it takes courage to forgive. Mahatma Gandhi urged us to meet the tragedies of life with what he called 'soul force'. It is true that forgiveness is not weak or naive. It requires courage and clarity, as the following words tell us:

If you want to see the heroic look
Look at those who can love
In return for hatred,
If you want to see the brave
Look at those who can forgive.

Survivors of the 9/11 World Trade Centre tragedy tell us that as the twin towers began to burn, they saw the following acts of courage, compassion, loving kindness and fearless service:

- One man slowly lowered a physically disabled colleague in a wheelchair and took him carefully, one step at a time, down sixty-eight floors, while all around them, people were rushing down, nearly mad with fear of losing their lives. The man in the wheelchair and his compassionate colleague got out in time.
- Yet another man stood at the landing outside his office, handing out wet paper towels to use as smoke masks to hundreds of people who descended before him.
- As panic stricken office workers poured out of the twin towers, teams of firemen and police rushed in fearlessly, motivated by their strong sense of duty and loving compassion.

True, there is suffering all around us. But wherever there is suffering, there are fearless, courageous, compassionate people who take on the sorrows of others as their own. They act without hesitation, they act selflessly, they care, they help, they heal.

Love is a mighty force indeed. And so it has been said: There is no hardship, no difficulty that love cannot conquer; no distance that love cannot span; no barrier that love cannot overcome.

4

What is Fear?

Psychiatrists tell us that only two fears are present at birth—the fear of falling and the fear of loud noises.

How is it then that we build up so many fears in later life? Does fear have an organic basis? Or is it simply built through the processes of our own unconscious?

People often think that fear is a destructive emotion. This is not entirely true. When we are afraid of things that truly threaten our security, such fear is protective. In fact, I would go so far as to say that man is fortunate to have learnt to fear certain things, or else, the human species would have been wiped out long ago.

Let us admit, fear is natural to human beings in many situations. It teaches us to be cautious and fosters our sense of self-preservation. It helps us create safeguards for ourselves. It is what keeps us safe and secure.

The dictionary defines fear as a painful emotion or passion excited by the expectation of evil, or the apprehension of impending danger. Synonyms for the word are apprehension, anxiety, alarm, dread.

'Fear is an uneasiness of the mind, upon the thought of future danger likely to befall us', wrote the philosopher John Locke.

The degrees of this painful emotion beginning with the most moderate may be expressed thus: *Apprehension, fear, dread, fright, terror.*

Let me try to explain by means of a simple example. Some of us may fancy the idea of riding a motorbike very fast, but we would be terrified if we are put in what circus artists call the 'Dome of death'—where a motorcyclist loops across and rides like a daredevil upside down within a steel dome. The motorcyclist probably experiences some fear, as does the lion tamer who steps into a cage full of lions, whip in hand. Fear is part of their job. You and I will not step into the cage or the dome. We would be terrified. However, we would love to go to the circus or the show and watch them perform!

This is considered normal behaviour.

There are a wide range of situations that spell danger and there are an equally wide range of fear responses. We accept our fears as normal fears or founded fears, when the fear is in proportion to the degree of danger in a situation. But if the fear response is out of proportion to the danger, it becomes an abnormal fear or a phobia.

Fear and anxiety are similar but there is one crucial difference between them—the cognitive component of fear—which is recognisable to us by perception or reasoning. It is the expectation of a clear and specific danger. On the other hand, anxiety is vague and unspecific. 'Something awful may happen to me!' 'Something terrible is about to happen…' is the typical reaction in anxiety or panic disorder. Fear is based on reality, or an exaggeration of a real danger. Anxiety is based on an irrational or formless danger.

5

Recognising Fear

I have said that fear permeates all aspects of our life on earth. Fear is not only present in our personalities, it seems to be woven into the very fabric of our institutions. Fear exists within the family—we are either afraid of some of our close relatives, or we fear for their safety and well-being. Fear exists in the workplace—the executive who is called to meet the big boss is often scared to death. Fear exists in our schools and colleges—the student who has not done his homework is frightened of the teacher, afraid of punishment. You can almost smell the fear in hospitals—patients are afraid of their own constitutions and the unknown, unforeseen health complications they may fall prey to. Sadly, children are afraid of parents and what's worse, some parents are actually afraid of their children!

Competition and rivalry have made professional life a veritable rat race. After all, a world fired by the spirit of rivalry and one-upmanship is a world built on the foundation of fear. Performance, evaluation, comparison—everything arouses fear. The fear of failure, the fear of losing a match or a contest, is one of the worst kinds of fear that haunts an individual. The stigma of failure makes us lose faith in ourselves. We are afraid of becoming unacceptable.

Though it is not possible to categorise or label it, I would like to mention the five basic types of fear identified by Dr Forrest Church:

- **Fright**—or instinctive fear that is associated with the body and designed to protect us from physical danger.

I recently read about a young lad who had lost his sense of touch and therefore, could feel no pain. On reading this, you might be tempted to exclaim, 'Isn't he lucky!' But the truth of the matter is that he was not so lucky. The absence of the symptoms of pain made his every action a potential hazard. He would simply not know if his muscles wore out, or if his limbs were fractured. If scalding water fell on his hands or he touched a live flame, there would be no jumping-out-of-the-skin sensation which makes people like you and me recoil almost instantly.

I know many people, who, at the first signs of discomfort in the chest—tightening, constriction, breathlessness or a flash of pain—reported to their doctor right away and actually managed to avoid a major heart attack. There is *that* in our brains, in our system, which warns us of impending danger or risk and cautions us to take care. Such a fear can be life-saving. It is through this cautionary impulse that careful drivers avert major accidents on the highway. It is through this inbuilt sense of fear that mothers and wives handle multiple chores in the kitchen safely, wielding knives and peelers and sharp implements, manoeuvring pots and pans on the hot cooking range, using gloves and dishcloths to move hot dishes in and out of ovens, and expertly dealing with oils and boiling liquids at high temperatures.

The Dalai Lama has confessed that he is afraid of flying. However, his responsibilities as a spiritual leader entail constant travel by flight. Therefore, he has come to terms with his fright; he has mustered the courage to tackle this fear with the determination: 'The more I fly, the less I sweat!'

All of us are familiar with these fright impulses—the sudden catch in the chest, a parched sensation in the mouth, cold and clammy hands. These are nerve signals sent out by the brain, meant to act as a warning to us. In turn, these signals trigger our safety responses; we act to protect ourselves, to avoid accidents. Intuition, intelligence and reflex action combine to guide us out of harm's way.

Therefore, the cautionary impulse of fright is actually good for us—we do hundreds of things safely because we know when we are afraid and we stop at the nick of time.

- **Worry**—is fear produced out of what we call our 'worst imaginings'.

Many years ago, when microwave ovens first came into the market, people began to raise several doubts about the new gadget. It is true that these ovens use microwave energy to cook or heat food very quickly; it is also true that these heat energy waves can be harmful to us if we are exposed to them for long periods. This is why microwave ovens have glass doors reinforced with a mesh so that no harmful heat waves can escape outside. Should the door be opened accidentally, the electrodes stop functioning automatically.

Many women took to the new gadget eagerly. It made life in the kitchen relatively easy for them. Constant watching and stirring could be avoided and cooking was so clean and quick! However, many others had serious reservations about the ovens. One woman remarked to a friend, 'I know someone who ate the food cooked in a microwave oven and this person developed a huge hole in the side of her face!'

This is what I call fear produced by the worst imagining!

I am deeply saddened when I read of the mistrust and suspicion that foreigners and people of different faiths and religions are subjected to, when they travel abroad. How sad it is when people imagine that someone with a different skin colour or a different way of combing their hair must be enemies or terrorists or evildoers.

An eminent entrepreneur from India, who belonged to the Islamic faith, spoke about how he was harassed and questioned and made to wait interminably at a foreign airport, just because he was a Muslim. He was not only one of the richest and most powerful men in industry, but a philanthropist and a deeply spiritual man who believed in simple, austere living.

Worry—fear of that which is absent—can wreak havoc on the human nervous system. If we do not handle worry firmly, we will fall victims to phobias, which are deep, inner obsessions.

- **Guilt**—is nothing but fear arising out of a troubled conscience.

There is a joke about a young man who was filling up an application for employment. He got to a question which read: 'Have you ever been arrested?' Taken aback for a minute, he wrote down firmly: 'No.'

The next question was actually meant to be answered only by those who had said 'yes' to the previous question. It only asked, 'Why?' (Meaning: Why were you arrested?)

The young man thought for a while and wrote down: 'Never been caught.'

Guilt is very often associated with the fear of being caught. It does not have to be the police trying to arrest you, it might also be the shame of being discovered to be a liar or a cheat; it might be the humiliation of people coming to know that one was mean or dishonest.

Unfortunately, guilt is associated with shame and secrecy. And when we have unpleasant secrets to keep, we often resort to lies. Thus, one thing leads to another and very often we find ourselves committing several wrongs to cover up the one initial wrong that we were guilty of in the first place.

This is why our elders said so wisely: 'Honesty is the best policy'. The best way to deal with guilt is to own up to our actions and face the consequences. Facing up to one wrong that we committed is far better than weaving a web of deceit to protect ourselves. Even when we are faced with some form of punishment, it still neutralises the terrible consequences of guilt.

Guilt can lead to terrible reactions, forming a vicious cycle of anger, shame and violence. There are thousands of poor working men in India, who are victims of alcoholism. At heart, they are ashamed and guilty, for having fallen prey to the dreadful demon of drinking, for throwing away their hard earned money on this vicious habit, for depriving their wives and children of the benefit of their income. Above all, they feel guilty about their own inherent weakness and cowardice which prevents them from conquering this vicious habit.

But what this guilt leads to is even more terrible. These men are hated and feared by their own children. They arrive home drunk every night and beat up their wives for no reason. Their behaviour is of course inexcusable, but they are in the grip of guilt and shame and are unable to control their own actions in their drunken state.

Now, there are several voluntary agencies offering free rehabilitation programmes for such people. But alcoholics lack the courage to take recourse to them easily, for they are locked in by their guilt, fear and shame. It is only when the fetters are thrown away that they can take a step in the right direction that can change their life for the better.

To name a guilty fear, to face up to it, is to win half the battle! Very often, those things that we are ashamed to acknowledge, those things that we are most reluctant to reveal to others, cause the worst kind of negative feelings associated with guilt. As I said earlier, guilt thrives on secrecy. We live in constant fear of being discovered; we are ashamed lest people should accuse us of our transgressions. We grow aggressive and prone to violent quarrels. When we remove the source of guilt, we free ourselves from shame and fear.

- **Insecurity**—is associated with the emotions. It is fear prompted by feelings of inadequacy.

A friend of mine is a professor at a well-known university. He told me that he had gone to his bank to withdraw some money. He wanted the amount in notes of different denominations—some notes of 500, some of 100, 50, 20 and 10.

The cashier counted out the notes quickly and efficiently, tied each bundle neatly with rubber bands and handed the cash over to him with a pleasant smile.

'You are truly amazing,' said my friend. 'Why, you counted all those different notes in a trice! I could never have done it so fast. Hats off to you!'

'Well, I could never ever have the courage to do what you do, so we are quits,' laughed the cashier.

'But what do I do that requires courage?' asked the professor in amazement. 'I am only a teacher you know.'

'Put me before a class of just twenty students,' said the cashier, 'and I shall go dumb with fear. You not only keep your wits about you, but lecture to them day after day. I could never utter a word before an audience to save my life!'

The cashier is one of thousands who is nervous about public speaking. Whenever surveys are conducted on what scares people most, public speaking invariably tops the list.

Even those who are accustomed to public speaking often admit that they are nervous and anxious as they walk to the podium. And if their eyes should fall upon a person who is talking, laughing or just not paying attention to what they are saying, they begin to feel that they are performing badly. If someone should actually walk away in the course of their talk, they even lose the train of their thought and begin to fumble.

In the good, old comic films starring Laurel and Hardy, Laurel often fixes his beady eyes on his small companion; coming under the glare of that scrutiny, Hardy becomes nervous, insecure and clumsy and messes up whatever he is doing. In no time at all, insecurity can lead to panic.

Insecurity attacks all kinds of people, not just the humble and ordinary. Popular stars are terrified of losing their ratings and fan following. Politicians are always insecure about winning the support of the public. Being allotted a marginal constituency—one in which election results may go in favour of any party—gives a candidate recurring nightmares.

There is a simple way to overcome insecurity. Most of the time, insecurity arises out of our obsession with the self—what we do, how we look, whether others like us, respect us, admire us. The best way to escape insecurity is to stop being absorbed in ourselves and start concentrating on others and their feelings and needs.

It is a sad fact of life that many people are obsessed about appearances. Once we start caring about deeper issues, our insecurity will vanish.

- **Dread**—is fear generated by the fundamental uncertainty of life.

Dr Church describes dread as 'a particularly crippling form of anxiety, driven by the desire to control things that lie beyond our control'.

When we feel we are losing control over our lives, our fears and anxieties are multiplied a thousandfold. We look at the future that lies ahead of us and we dread to contemplate it. Our worries and negative feelings are all projected on to the giant screen of the future and we see our lives in a mess!

This leads us on to depression—one of the most common ailments associated with our times. Depression represents the conquest of hopelessness over hope. It cuts us off from everything that can help us and save us, plunging us deeper and deeper into isolation and alienation. It drives peace and joy out of our very existence.

Human life is such that there will be times when we are overwhelmed by defeat, pain or suffering. At such times, our best recourse is to turn to someone, a friend who can offer us a shoulder to lean on. And who better than the Friend of the friendless and forlorn, He who has been called Mata, *Pita, Bandhu, Sakha*—Mother, Father, Relative and Friend, all rolled into One!

6

FAITH GIVES YOU COURAGE

I can never forget the sweet, serene face of a child whom I saw several decades ago when I was on board the *SS Versova*, travelling from Bombay to Karachi. Suddenly, a terrible storm arose at sea. Thick, dark clouds appeared in the sky, the sun hid behind the gathering clouds and the day grew dark. Huge waves rose, dashing against the steamer, which was tossed about as if it were no more than a paper boat.

All the passengers on board were terrified. It seemed as if we were doomed to a watery grave. Amid all the commotion and confusion on deck, I saw a little child—a boy who was barely six-years old sitting in a corner—calm, serene, undisturbed by the shrieking winds and the rolling waves.

At that time, I was about ten-years old. Though I was affected by the fear of my fellow passengers, I could not help but marvel at the unruffled serenity that I beheld on the child's face.

I said to him gently, 'It looks as if the steamer is about to sink. Are you not afraid?'

With a cherubic smile he answered, 'What have I to fear when my mother is near?'

I can never forget those words. When I am caught in the depths of despair and sorrow, I have repeated those words to myself, repeated them again and again, until I felt relieved: 'What have I to fear when my mother is near?'

Our Mother—the Mother Divine is so near to each one of us. Closer is She than our breath and nearer even than our hands and feet. Alas! It is we who have turned our faces away from Her. In our shouts and shows, in our futile engagements and activities, in our business and commerce, we have forgotten Her!

We have lost our childlike spirit. To be childlike is to rejoice in life, to love and laugh, to be free from care and anxiety. The trouble is that we think we have grown up and no longer need the Mother's loving care. We need to become children again, friendly and loving towards all, never fearful, never insecure.

We need to contact the Mother. But we must also remember that it is impossible for us to find Her through our own efforts and endeavour. It is only through Her own grace that we may find Her!

This grace may be obtained through meditation, prayer and constant repetition of the Mother's name. Writing the name, again and again, is of great help. To start with, it might seem mechanical, but as you grow in concentration, writing the name becomes a source of indescribable joy. As you keep on writing the name, again and again, one blessed day, you lose yourself and you find the Mother! That is all that matters.

'You are not alone, O Arjuna!' said Sri Krishna to his beloved disciple in the Gita. 'I am with you, within you, all around you. Whatever you eat, whatever you give, whatever you do, do it as an offering unto Me!'

Thus, may our petty wills be blended with the Divine will. And in the measure in which our wills are blended with the will of God, in that measure do we grow in strength, confidence and hope. Then it is that fear vanishes from our life, as mist before the morning sun. And we move through life trusting every ray of sunshine and every drop of rain, every rose and every thorn, every stone and every grain of sand, every river and every rock, trusting the sun and moon and stars, trusting thunder and storm, trusting everything and everyone!

7

How to Conquer Fear

'The mind is its own place,' wrote Milton, 'and in itself, can create a heaven of hell, a hell of heaven.' How true! The mind can create strife and conflict; it can also create peace. If we are to live a life of peace and attain freedom from fear, we must discover peace within ourselves. We must be fearless in the mind.

It is no easy task to still the mind. A mind that is wandering and restless is like a disturbed lake; waves are constantly surging on its surface and it cannot reflect the stillness of the sky. When we control our thoughts, we still the mind and it becomes capable of beautiful, elevating reflections—reflections of the divine light within us.

Many people often ask me why it is necessary to control the mind. 'What's the use of going blank?' they want to know. 'Is it necessary for me to become a stone? Shouldn't I feel for people? Shouldn't I be conscious of my responsibilities to others?'

Certainly, you must feel for others and feel for yourself. It is not recommended that you stop thinking or feeling when you learn to control the mind. When you have conquered the mind, when you have achieved inner tranquillity, you will begin to create new, beautiful, positive thoughts and feelings. Once this is achieved, even if negative thoughts arise in the mind, they cannot affect your inner calm and peace. This is why spiritually awakened men do not suffer from fear, worry, anxiety or restlessness.

The three qualities at play in nature are also at play in the mind. Thus, *Tamas* is total lethargy and inaction. *Rajas* is the opposite extreme—too much activity and restlessness. *Sattva*, the desirable state, is tranquillity when both sides are well balanced. When we achieve this state of focused activity and complete mental relaxation, we achieve tranquillity of mind.

Selfish thoughts are at the root of forces that disturb the mind. Selfish thoughts pave the way for stress, worry, anxiety, disappointment and fear. These thoughts need not be suppressed; they should be replaced with positive, selfless ones.

This will teach you what to do about your fears and phobias. There are two options open to you. One is to submit to your fears, allow yourself to be overwhelmed by them, making your life miserable in the process. I'm afraid very many people adopt this course. They live with their fears all their lives, suffering needless misery and anxiety. What a great pity this is!

The other option—the wiser alternative—is to conquer your fears, with God's help. When you do this, you achieve a remarkable victory that can change your life. This victory is not the sole prerogative of the holy, the mighty and the brave. All of us have the potential to achieve it.

This is not easy. Fear is a tenacious beast. It is like a potent poison that quickly circulates through the entire system, paralysing the will.

And fear is a merciless master. It is one of the greatest foes known to man. Overcome fear the moment it raises its head—or it will overpower you! Strike fear with the weapon of the spirit—the word of God. Utter the name that is dear to you—Krishna, Rama, Jesus, Buddha, Allah, Nanak. Utter it again and again! Utter it in childlike faith and He whom you call will surely rush to your aid.

Very often, I repeat the following prayer from one of the songs composed by my Beloved Master, Sadhu Vaswani:

The sea is vast, my skiff is small:
I trust in Thee, who guard'st all!

The spoken word has the power to fight all evil—temptation, sin, anger and fear. This is why many people learn to recite a sacred mantra that is dear to them. A mantra is not just a word; its profound sound vibrations have the mystic power to align the mind and harmonise it. We believe that these sacred mantras were first heard in the divine consciousness of our ancient rishis as they sat in deep meditation. Since then, these mantras have been handed down for generations by great spiritual masters for the benefit of all humanity. By repeating these mantras constantly, you will create beautiful, positive vibrations within yourself, positively influencing your physical, emotional, intellectual and spiritual well-being. The *pranava* mantra, the cosmic sound which we represent as Om, has multiple aspects of divine vibration. In fact, many wise men feel that all mantras are only different facets of Om.

Many gurus give a particular mantra or naam for their students to recite and meditate on. But there are also general mantras which all of us can repeat, such as *Om, Hari Om,* or *Om Shanti.*

If you are not able to recite a mantra, you can recite a poem or a prayer which will sustain your strength and help you conquer fear. I know many people who have received strength and solace from that immortal hymn, *Abide with Me!*

Abide with me! Fast falls the eventide:
The darkness deepens: Lord, with me abide!
When other helpers fail, and comforts flee,
Help of the helpless, O abide with me!

Then there are the beautiful lines of Cardinal Newman, which I have found inspiring:

Lead kindly Light, amid th' encircling gloom
Lead Thou me on!
The night is dark, and I am far from home
Lead Thou me on!

I have repeated these lines from a poem by Ella Wheeler Wilcox again and again:

I will not doubt though all my ships at sea
Come drifting home with broken masts and sails
I shall believe the Hand which never fails
From seeking evil worketh good for me:
And though I weep because those sails are battered,
Still will I cry, while my best hopes lie shattered,
'I trust in Thee!'

Recite these or other lines, which may have a special appeal for you; recite them again and again, until fear departs and you feel as strong as steel.

As I said, fear is a tenacious beast that clings to the intricate webs of your consciousness. How can you free yourself from its clutches? The first step is to become aware that fear, like all other human weaknesses, is removable. It was not put into you by God. You acquired it somewhere along the way; you took it upon yourself, or it was put into you by the environment in which you live. Whatever it was, fear is removable.

Are you prone to anger and irritation? These can be removed. Are you given to bouts of depression and despair? These are removable. Do you suffer from inferiority complex? It is also removable.

The important thing is for you to realise that you are not condemned to live with fear all your life. It is entirely removable! Once you internalise this fact, you can begin to work on the process of actually removing your fear. This is possible through self-discipline.

8

WITNESS OF THE GREAT ONES

Is not fearlessness the first essential condition for spiritual growth? Sri Adi Shankaracharya, one of the greatest intellectuals of all times, urged that he, who would walk the way of the spirit must have *vajrahridaya*, a heart strong as a thunderbolt.

When Swami Vivekananda returned from America and embarked upon his work of regeneration in India, the one message which he delivered to the people as he travelled from town to town, from village to village, in this ancient land of heroes and sages, was this: 'Be bold! Be fearless!'

Anyone who reads Swamiji's words is sure to feel a thrill, a sense of power, even today. Here are a few words which I love to recall:

> Stand up, be bold, be strong! Strength is life, weakness is death. Weakness is the one cause of suffering. We become miserable because we are weak. We lie, steal, kill and commit other crimes, because we

> are weak. We suffer, because we are weak. Where there is nothing to weaken us, there is no death, no sorrow.

Let me narrate to you a wonderful incident from the life of Swami Vivekananda, which I have found moving. Swamiji was then in America, addressing large audiences on the wisdom of India's rishis and sages. He emphasised the idea that the way of the spirit was not for weaklings; the way is for heroes, for those who would be fearless in the face of every calamity, even death.

Now, there were a few young men who wished to put the Swami to the test. After all, they said to themselves, we know many men who are wonderful preachers, but their own lives do not bear witness to what they teach. Perhaps Swami Vivekananda belonged to the same class!

They invited him to deliver a lecture in their association. He gladly agreed and went to their meeting. He spoke to them of faith in God, which he saw as the secret of the true life. The man of faith, he emphasised, was fearless in the face of difficulty and danger.

Suddenly, pistol shots rang out in the crowded hall. Bullets whizzed past Swamiji, almost grazing his ears. Pandemonium broke out among the audience. Men rushed out of the hall, women began to scream in fear, some people fainted and fell to the ground.

In the midst of all this confusion, one man stood firm, immovable as a rock, fearless and bold—Swamiji himself. He knew that if the bullet was not meant for him, it could not touch him; if it was meant for him, it would seek him out even if he were protected by a thousand bodyguards.

After a while the gunshots ceased. Swamiji picked up the thread of the talk where he had left it just a minute ago—a long minute, it had seemed. Drawn by the magnetism of his voice, those who had fled returned to their seats, others woke up from their fainting fits. Normalcy was restored at the meeting and it seemed as if nothing untoward had taken place there at all.

When the lecture was over, the young men met Swami Vivekananda. 'Please forgive us,' they begged him. 'We had the shots fired to see if you were really fearless. Your courage and confidence have put us to shame. You must surely be the most fearless man on earth! Pray forgive us!'

Purna was one of Buddha's devoted disciples. He was inspired to spread his master's message among the people of Sonapranta. Now it was well known that the people of Sonapranta were wild and ferocious. No preacher's life was safe in their country. Puma's plan appeared preposterous to many of his fellow bhikkus, who feared for his life.

But Purna was a man of faith; there was no fear in his heart, for it was filled through and through with love for all living creatures and profound compassion for those who live in the darkness of ignorance.

He went to the Buddha for his blessings. The Master said to him, 'Purna, you know so well that the people of Sonapranta are wild and ferocious, they insult and slander one another and are given to uncontrollable fits of anger. If they insult you and abuse you and vent their wrath on you, what will you do?'

'If they abuse me and insult me, Master,' said Purna, 'I shall still think them to be kind and friendly, since they do not beat me or stone me.'

'And what if they beat you or stone you?'

'I would still regard them as being kind, since they do not attack me with weapons.'

'And if,' said the Buddha, 'they should attack you with weapons?'

'Then, too,' answered Purna, 'I would regard them as kind and friendly, since they do not kill me.'

'And what if they kill you, Purna?'

'Even if they kill me, Master,' said Purna, 'I shall thank them at the moment of my death, for they will liberate me from the limitations of the body and the bonds of human life!'

The Buddha was well pleased with Purna. 'You are gifted with the greatest gentleness and patience,' he said. 'You may go and dwell among the people of Sonapranta. Show them the way to be free, even as you are free!'

Blessed was Purna! He was free, he was fearless and he showed the people of Sonapranta how to be as he was. It is not the way of rushing after pleasure, accumulating possessions or acquiring earthly power. It is not the way of *preya*—the smooth and slippery way of ease and comfort. It is the way of *shreya*—the tough and difficult path. But it is the path that brings in you the awareness that you are very near and dear to God.

'Are not five sparrows sold for two farthings?' asked Jesus. 'And not one of them is forgotten in the sight of God. Fear not, ye are of more value than many sparrows!'

The great German poet Goethe was particularly fond of a story relating to Jesus and his disciples. Peter the fisherman, the foremost among the disciples, once said to Christ, 'Master, how is it that you can walk on the waters, and we cannot?'

Jesus answered, 'Because I have faith!'

Peter protested, 'But we have faith in you too!'

'Then follow me,' said Jesus and stepped on the water. Peter followed him—and he actually walked upon the waters behind his Master!

They had not gone very far when a huge wave arose before them. Peter cried out, 'Master, save me! I am about to drown!'

'Why are you afraid?' asked Jesus.

'I saw the huge wave, Master,' Peter replied, 'and fear entered my heart!'

Jesus said to him, 'You feared the wave; you did not fear the Lord of the waves!'

I recall a moving incident in the life of Muhammad, the great prophet of Islam, often retold. He learnt from his friends that his life was in danger and that fierce men had been sent out to kill him under the cover of night. Muhammad was constrained to leave his home at that dark hour. With him was his friend and faithful follower, Abu Bakr.

In hot pursuit of these two devoted servants of God, were the men who were out to kill Muhammad. They rode strong steeds and in their hands they carried drawn swords and sharp spears.

Abu Bakr saw them from a distance and was terribly frightened. In abject terror, he said to Muhammad, 'They are coming! They will be upon us soon. They will slay us with their sharp swords. Our bodies will lie on the desert sands to be devoured by wild animals.'

Muhammad was silent. In his heart he felt sure that God was with them and that they were safe.

Nearby was a cave. Muhammad and Abu Bakr hid themselves in the depths of the cave. The party of persecutors rode up after some time. They halted at the mouth of the cave. Their leader suspected that Muhammad may be hiding inside the cave.

Abu Bakr began to tremble like a leaf in the wind. 'What shall we do now?' he whispered. 'There are so many of them and we are only two!'

Quietly answered Muhammad, 'Not so, my friend! We are not two, but three. The third is Allah! And when He is near, we need not fear.'

The story goes on to tell us that a miracle happened and they were saved. But what I would like to emphasise is the faith of Muhammad, which enables him to overcome fear: 'The third is Allah and when He is near, we need not fear!'

Sant Eknath was a disciple of Janardhan Swami. The Swami was then a Governor in charge of a fort. Once a week, Janardhan Swami devoted a whole day to silence, meditation and communion with the Divine.

Taking advantage of this, a Muslim king decided to attack the fort and capture it on the day of Janardhan's weekly retreat. He was sure that he could conquer the fort with ease, while the Governor sat in prayer and meditation.

At that time, Sant Eknath was a young boy of just sixteen or seventeen years. He heard of the enemy's onslaught, but was unafraid. He knew that it was his responsibility to defend the fort, while his guru was in dhyana. The young man entered the guru's room, put on the guru's armour and took up his sword. He mounted his guru's horse and led his army forward. He won the battle, routed the enemy, sent him fleeing and returned to the fort, victorious.

Quietly, he stabled the horse, returned the armour and the sword to the guru's room and attended the evening satsang in the guru's presence, without uttering a word about his own fearless feat! Such was his spiritual strength that he had been able to take on the burden of his guru at that tender age.

My Beloved Master, Sadhu Vaswani, was barely three or four-years old when this incident happened. It was a sultry afternoon and he stood outside his house, gazing at the few passers-by.

It was the siesta hour. People were dozing inside their homes and the whole locality wore a deserted look.

Suddenly, a fierce-looking, huge Pathan appeared before the child. Before he could even realise what was happening, the child felt a rough hand catch hold of him by the scruff of the neck and he was thrust into a deep pit of darkness.

It took the child a long time to understand what was happening. He was being spirited away, hidden in the Pathan's flowing robes!

'Help me, help me God!' he prayed fervently. 'Save me from this darkness!'

A few passers-by began to eye the Pathan suspiciously. His awkward movement and the mysterious bulk in his garment caught their eye, for the child had begun to struggle.

'Hey, what's up?' one of them called out.

Realising that he was being watched, the Pathan darted into a doorway. Adroitly pulling the child out, he left him on the doorstep and vanished as suddenly as he had appeared.

Referring to this incident, Sadhu Vaswani said later, 'We are in the darkness of *avidya*—ignorance. We need to offer, again and again, the prayer of the ancient rishi—*Tamaso ma jyotir gamaya*. O Lord, out of darkness, lead me into light!'

Mohandas was extremely timid and fearful as a child. The slightest noise would scare him—a shadow falling in the darkness would fill him with fright. He would not even go from one room to another in the night.

The maidservant who took care of him said to him, one day, 'Mohan! Why are you so afraid? Don't you know that Lord Rama is always with you, guiding you, guarding you, watching your every step and protecting you at all times? Whenever you are afraid, just repeat His name. He is all-powerful. He will look after you!'

Young Mohandas began to repeat the sacred 'Rama Naam' from that day onwards. He found that his fear vanished like mist before the morning sun.

And this young boy grew up to be the great-souled leader who defied the might of the world's greatest colonial power. Fearlessness and moral courage enabled him to lead his country to glorious freedom. Ultimately, he faced the bullets of an assassin with the sacred 'Rama Naam' on his lips!

Yes, he was Mahatma Gandhi, the apostle of non-violence. He taught us that ahimsa was also *abhaya*—fearlessness.

PART II

How We Can Kill Fear

1

Nothing is as Bad as Fear Itself

I recall the words of the great statesman, American President Franklin D Roosevelt, who delivered a memorable inaugural address on 4 March 1933 at a time when America was facing the worst economic depression in her history.

> Let me assert my firm belief that the only thing we have to fear is fear itself—nameless, unreasoning terror which paralyses efforts needed to convert retreat into advance.

'No more vital utterance was ever made by a President of the United States,' read an editorial next morning. Indeed, the President seemed to have touched the very hearts of the people with his memorable words.

In a lesser known but equally powerful Congressional address delivered on 6 January 1941, President Roosevelt proclaimed four basic freedoms—

freedom of speech, freedom of worship, freedom from want and freedom from fear. The significant thing was that he included freedom from fear as something essential and fundamental to human happiness. He made it clear that fear was one of the greatest enemies of a free nation and free people. Himself a victim of the dreaded polio which made him unable to walk without support, he also knew that fear can be more paralysing, more crippling than polio.

A man who was travelling on a lonely road was set upon by bandits who beat him up severely and robbed him of all his possessions. They bound his hands and feet and dragged him into the dark depths of a forest. Here they gagged him and blindfolded him, tied him to a rope and suspended him from a height.

'You are now hanging over the brink of a giddy precipice,' they told him. 'The moment you let go of this rope, you will be dashed to pieces on the rocks below.' And with those words they left him.

He was filled with terror at the impending doom. He clung on for dear life to the rope which swung hither and thither. He gave in to despair as his grip failed, and he fell—barely six inches, landing on the comforting solidity of mother earth! The grass was soft and moist to his touch and the earth smelt clean and refreshing. Quickly he untied his blindfold. The robbers had played a cruel trick on him and left him hanging in fear, so that they could make good their escape. When he let go, he was not letting go of his life, but only his fear!

Fort Alcan was a historical settlement of early European migrants in British Columbia, Canada. When Fort Alcan was abandoned after centuries as it had become old and decrepit, needy miners and other settlers in the area began to strip the place for anything valuable that they could lay their hands on, like lumber, electrical appliances, plumbing and hardware. While dismantling the jail in the settlement, they found mighty locks, reinforced steel doors, thick steel bars covering the windows and so on. But the walls of the prison were made of wallboard of clay and paper, merely painted to resemble iron. A good old push against the walls by a man built like a footballer—and the 'iron walls' would have collapsed. But the amazing thing was that no one ever tried it—no one thought it was possible!

Alas, many of us are prisoners of fear, like the wretched inmates of Fort Alcan prison. We do not know our strength and do not realise that fear is nothing when we push against it and set it aside.

In the cold northern stretches of Europe, Canada and Russia, which are close to the Arctic Circle, temperatures fall far below zero degree Celsius in winter and rivers and ponds freeze completely. Children ski and play on the frozen surfaces of these rivers and lakes and people cross them walking, to get to the other side.

On a dark, winter night, a man had to cross a wide frozen river. The people living on the riverbank assured him that it was perfectly safe to do so, since the river would stay frozen for weeks together. In fact, several people crossed back and forth constantly, walking on the solid ice.

The traveller decided to cross over, but he decided to crawl as slowly as he could, so that he could feel the ice and move cautiously. When he was near the middle of the frozen stream, he was startled by a sound in the distance and caught sight of a tall and hefty man driving a team of four horses which were pulling a heavy load of pig iron. 'Giddyap! Giddyap!' he urged the horses forward. The whole contraption sped across the surface of the river, as the man watched, crouching on all fours—and there was not the least sign of a crack in the ice!

The man realised how foolish he had been to fear and crawl as he had done.

A steamer full of passengers was moving along the St Lawrence river. It was early evening and the river was suddenly enveloped in a thick fog that brought visibility down to nil. However, the boat was travelling ahead at full speed despite the heavy fog encircling it.

Some of the passengers became alarmed. Angrily, they complained to the first mate that the boat should be slowed down at once.

'Oh, don't be afraid!' the mate assured them with a smile. 'The fog you see around lies very low; the captain is high above the fog at his post. He can see where we are going!'

A business executive was flying long distance across the Pacific. A little boy travelling home for his holidays was seated next to him. As the passengers were dozing after an excellent lunch, there was an urgent message from the pilot to fasten their seat belts as the plane was about to run into stormy weather, heavy rain and wind. Despite the enormous size of the plane and the power of its engines, the flight was jolted badly.

The boy became desperately afraid and clung to the older man's arms. On his part, the man stroked the boy's head gently to reassure him.

'Aren't you afraid?' whispered the boy, as the plane dipped all of a sudden.

'No!' laughed the man. 'This is real fun, isn't it? Aren't you enjoying yourself?'

An immediate change came over the little boy. His fear and tension left him and he too, began to enjoy the 'fun', laughing and squealing delightedly as the plane dipped and swayed.

The executive had taught the young one a valuable lesson in the art of living!

'Cowards die many deaths, the brave die but once,' goes the proverb. It's true, that each of us has only one life, but how many of us 'die a thousand deaths' in fear and nervousness.

The ancient legends tell us the story of a brave warrior, who once arrived at a village, to find the people there living in abject terror.

The village was surrounded by a marsh covered with wild undergrowth and thick mangroves. Hidden in the marshes lived five dreadful birds of prey—their beaks stronger and sharper than swords of steel. Fierce and hideous were these man-eating birds. Every now and then, they would fly out of the marsh with a great fluttering of their weapon-like wings, swoop down on the hapless villagers, attacking them ferociously and even carrying away little babies in their beaks. In vain did the villagers try to rid themselves of these predatory birds. They were too swift and too strong to be killed by arrows. The marsh would not allow traps to be laid for them—for when men walked over the marsh, they were caught in the slough.

The villagers rejoiced to see the brave warrior. 'O helper of the helpless ones, we are indeed delighted to see you here!' they said to him. 'We live in constant fear. Long and weary has been our wait for our saviour. Do something for us!'

The brave warrior thought long and hard. He was anxious to help the poor, fear-stricken villagers but he could think of no way to capture the huge birds, dead or alive.

At long last, a plan materialised in his mind. He called the villagers and explained what he was about to do. The villagers would carry cymbals, drums and any other instruments which they could lay hands on and walk in a long procession to the marsh. The warrior would lead them, carrying the loudest and largest of cymbals. They would all plug their ears with cotton so that they would not be deafened by the sound.

The villagers did as they were told and arrived at the marsh. The warrior clanged his giant cymbals again and again, and the villagers sang the name of God at the top of their voices to keep their terror at bay.

Confused by the monstrous deafening clangour, the ravenous birds came out of their hiding places and flew at them wildly flapping their wings. Totally confused and bemused by the noise, they began to screech horribly. Then, frightened out of their wits, they flew away in frantic hurry, never to return again.

In sheer joy, the village folk began to dance and sing. 'Victory to the brave warrior!' they chanted. 'He conquered the predators!'

'You conquered your fear and that drove the birds away,' laughed the warrior. 'All victory to God, whose unprofitable servant I am!'

We are told that abstract thoughts (such as those that generate fear) arise from the higher brain centres, whereas the impulses that generate physical activity (such as walking, exercise and playing games) come from the lower brain centres. There was a talk some time back that surgeons had devised a new operation by which portions of the frontal lobe of the brain could be removed in an effort to literally cut away fear and worry. We cannot comment on the scientific or practical value of the operation, but I cannot help thinking what a good thing it would be if we could just go to a doctor and have those destructive parts of our brain removed which cause havoc in our lives by producing poisonous fear and worry, just as we have our tonsils or appendix removed!

However, it seems to me that if we keep those lower centres of our brain busy with physical activity, the trouble caused by the higher centres would certainly abate in proportion! In other words, we would be better off expending our physical energy in walking and other activities rather than spending our mental energy indulging in useless fears.

Mary Ellen Chase, an American scholar, tells us that manual labour is 'not only good and decent for its own sake, but also for straightening out one's thoughts'. She adds, 'The best antidote I know for a confused head or tangled emotions is to work with one's hands. To scrub a floor has alleviated many a broken heart and to wash and iron one's clothes has brought order and clarity to many a perplexed and anxious mind.'

A young man was victim to obsessive and recurrent fear. He approached a well-known psychiatrist to solve his problem. Do you know one of the measures prescribed by the psychiatrist? He advised the young man to jog every night till he was weary and tired for this would ensure that he fell soundly asleep, thus, effectively conquering his fears.

When India's elderly statesman, Chakravarti Rajagopalachari went to London, he was mightily impressed with the neon signs and hoardings that proclaimed: 'Take Courage!' and remarked to his hosts that he found them inspiring and uplifting.

It is a different matter altogether that his hosts were too embarrassed to tell him that 'Courage' was nothing but a popular brand of beer and the 'inspiring' signs were only exhorting people to drink more of it!

Jokes apart, a stout heart and courageous spirit are vital if we are to live a life free from fear. Dr Samuel Johnson knew this well, which is why he remarked that courage was the primary virtue. 'Unless a man has that virtue,' he wrote, 'he has no security for preserving any other'.

An Arabic folk tale tells us that a wise old man travelling on the desert road to Baghdad met the figure of Pestilence hurrying ahead of him.

'Why are you in such a haste to reach Baghdad?' asked the old man.

'I am due to take five thousand lives in the city,' Pestilence replied, before it went away.

Later, on the return journey, they chanced to meet again. 'You lied to me,' said the old man reproachfully. 'You said you would take five thousand lives, but you took away ten thousand instead.'

'I did not do it!' Pestilence swore. 'I took five thousand and not one more; it was Fear who killed the rest!'

Truly, fear destroys the soul, sapping our will to live. The Persian poet Hafiz expresses this in memorable words when he tells us:

Fear is the cheapest room in the house.
I'd like to see you in better living conditions.

2

Cultivate the Will to Be Free of Fear

Let me begin this chapter with the inspiring words of India's national poet, Rabindranath Tagore:

This is my prayer to You, my Lord—strike,
Strike at the root of penury in my heart.
Give me the strength lightly to bear my joys and sorrows.
Give me the strength to make my love fruitful in service.
Give me the strength never to disown the poor
Or bend my knees before insolent might.
Give me the strength to raise my mind high above daily trifles
And give me the strength to surrender my strength to Your will with love.

Freedom from fear is achieved through perseverance, tenacity and sheer will power. Have you heard about the teacher who asked the smartest boy in class, 'Tell me Hari, what is the difference between perseverance and obstinacy?'

The clever lad replied, 'One is a strong will, and the other is a strong *wont*.'

Let me tell you the story of two frogs that fell into a bucket of cream. At first they were bemused, but unafraid. Valiantly, they tried their best to get out of the sticky fluid by climbing up the side of the slippery bucket. But it was impossible. When they climbed eight inches, they slipped back ten inches.

One of the frogs panicked. 'We will never make it out of here alive,' he sobbed. 'I give up. I can't take it anymore.' In his fear and frustration, he got drowned in the cream.

The other frog was resolute and determined. 'I shan't be afraid,' he told himself, 'I shall find my way out. I shall live!' He went on and on, kicking with his back legs and climbing with his front legs. He fell back every time, but did not give up his effort.

Suddenly, he found that he hit something hard as he fell back on the cream. He turned to see what it was and discovered to his surprise that his kicking had churned up a sizable lump of butter! Quickly, he jumped on top of it and leaped out to safety.

A Chinese proverb tells us: 'The man who dislodged the mountain began by carrying away small stones.' How true! What is required is that we must not be daunted by the circumstances around us and the obstacles ahead of us.

When Columbus set out on his historic voyage which culminated in the discovery of America, he certainly had to sail through rough weather, figuratively speaking. As they kept sailing, day after day, across the vast Atlantic Ocean, no land appeared. The sailors threatened mutiny and demanded that the ships should turn back. Columbus's life was at risk from the fierce men. But he was undaunted. He was determined to pursue his goal and each day, he would enter just two words in the captain's log book: 'Sailed on.'

There is a romantic story told to us of the father and mother of Thomas Becket, martyr and saint of England. Gilbert Becket, Thomas's father, had made a pilgrimage to the holy land in his youth. Here he was captured by a Saracen, who imprisoned him in his castle. The only daughter of the Saracen chief fell in love with Gilbert. She was young, fair and beautiful. Gilbert promised to marry her if she would come to England with him, for he too loved her deeply. However, he soon found the opportunity to escape from the Saracen's clutches. When he returned to England, he forgot all about the young girl who had given her heart to him.

However, the girl did not forget him so easily. She was determined to leave her father's house in disguise and find her way across to England. Her friends were taken aback by her decision, for in those days—this was eight hundred years ago—women did not set out alone in search of their lovers, especially those whose very language and address was unknown to them!

The girl was not afraid. She knew just two English words—London and Gilbert. She travelled to the coast and went among the ships in the wharf, saying, 'London, London'. Sailors led her to a ship which was about to sail for London and she paid for her passage with some of her jewels.

Having arrived in London (which was then only a small town), she walked across the streets, calling out, 'Gilbert! Gilbert!' One of Becket's servants, who had been imprisoned with his master, saw her and rushed to inform his master. 'Master, master!' he said, 'As I live, the Saracen girl is here in London! I saw her walking up and down, calling out your name!'

Gilbert hurried to find her. When she saw him, she wept tears of joy and fainted in his loving arms. It was her will and determination that had made her brave unknown dangers and seek her lover. They were married soon after.

Only they can conquer fear who have willed themselves to do so!

When the French philosopher, Jean-Jacques Rousseau published his works, he was hunted and hounded from one place to another because of his radical opinions. Even people who knew him and respected his intellect, were afraid to offer him refuge in their homes.

Voltaire heard of Rousseau's plight and invited him to come and live in his home. When Rousseau accepted the offer gratefully, Voltaire embraced him and said, 'I may not agree with your views, but I will fight to the death for your right to say what you think.'

Voltaire was a man who was prepared to stand up and be counted. He was not afraid to defend what he believed in!

The yearning for freedom—political, social, intellectual, economic or religious—is embedded so deeply in men, that people even risk their lives to achieve it. This is the reason why *abhaya* or fearlessness has been the hallmark of the world's greatest intellectuals, martyrs and saints. This was why Socrates drank hemlock, calmly and dispassionately. This was why Christ allowed himself to be crucified. This was why Mahatma Gandhi faced his assassin's bullets with the name of the Lord on his lips. These great souls had cultivated the will to be unafraid, the will to conquer fear at all cost.

In his early days as the Messenger of Allah, Prophet Muhammad faced the enmity and hostility of certain powerful men. Among his chief enemies were the powerful leaders of the Koreishi tribe who spread slander against him and incited people to stone him and attack him wherever he went.

The Prophet's uncle Abu Talib, an old man, was alarmed by the antagonism and hatred that his nephew had to face. In his anxiety and fear, he said to the Prophet, 'My dear nephew, the Koreishites are strong and powerful and they hate you! Heed my words: Fear their power; do not provoke their wrath. Give up your preaching and return to your trade, I entreat you!'

Prophet Muhammad was unafraid. To the old uncle whom he loved and respected, Muhammad said gently but firmly, 'Be not afraid for me. God will help me to stand by the truth, or give me death!'

Whenever Sadhu Vaswani narrated this story to us, he would exclaim, 'Truth, though she lead me to the gallows! Truth, though she take me through the fire!'

'People do not lack strength,' said Victor Hugo. 'They lack will.'

A missionary society was deeply impressed by the courageous devotion of Dr Livingstone's work in Africa. Expressing their appreciation for his efforts, they wrote to him: 'Tell us if there is a good road to where you are. We will then send other men to help you.'

Livingstone replied, 'If you have men who will only come here if there is a good road, they are of no use to me. I want men with will, who won't hesitate to come here even if there is no road at all!'

A very wise man once wrote: Let us not pray for easy lives. Let us pray that we may become stronger. Let us not pray for tasks equal to our powers. Let us pray for powers equal to our tasks.

Napoleon was facing an imminent defeat in one of his many battles. His men were falling back in disorder and disarray. Napoleon's eyes fell on a young drummer boy who was following him fearlessly. 'Beat a retreat!' he ordered hastily.

Saluting smartly, the heroic drummer boy replied, 'Sir, you have never taught me to beat a retreat. I can only beat a charge!'

Napoleon's eyes shone with courage. 'Well then, beat a charge, drummer boy!' he said. The boy did as he was told and a seeming defeat was turned into victory.

'Onward, forward, Godward!' was the spiritual exhortation of my master, Sadhu Vaswani. Real progress is only possible when we have the will power to pursue our chosen goals fearlessly.

Film stars, pop singers and celebrities from show business often feel insecure about their future, their popularity among the public, their remuneration and the offers they receive. Many of them are forced to make professional and ethical compromises to maintain their 'ratings' at the box office.

Pat Boone was a popular singer who was resolute enough never to compromise his beliefs and values. He was offered thousands of dollars in those days to appear in three TV shows. He turned down the lucrative offers without second thoughts for these programmes were sponsored by cigarette manufacturers and alcohol sellers. 'I am personally opposed to both smoking and drinking,' he said. 'I do not want to influence anyone to take to these habits.'

Pat Boone was unafraid of losing money or indeed of his ratings dropping. The thought of turning down lucrative contracts did not weaken his will power; he refused to compromise his ideals.

When Captain Cook and his team set out on their expedition to discover the North Pole, they were caught in a severe blizzard while still miles away from their encampment. Dr Daniel Solander, a Swedish naturalist who accompanied them, delivered a severe warning to the men. 'I have experienced such blizzards before,' he said. 'You have not. Now mark my words, for your lives depend upon it. Set your mind resolutely on returning to camp. Even a minute's rest is dangerous in these conditions.'

The men began to plod on. Conditions were indeed severe and extreme. Some men began to panic. Others complained of exhaustion.

'Keep moving!' ordered the quick-tempered doctor. 'This is a chance to see the stuff you are made of. Keep moving!'

The truth was, as their blood grew cold, the men asked to be allowed to rest, for they were afraid that if they moved ahead, they might fall down with strain. But the doctor knew that the wish to stop was the first symptom of the slowing down of blood circulation. To yield to it would mean death! So he would not allow them to rest even for a moment. He urged them on, at times with blows, at times with the bayonet.

The party plodded on through the icy winds and the driving snow. The frost cut into their skin. But their minds were set on their goals. Their stout hearts held on. After the first hour, no man ever expressed the wish to stop. If any of them felt a longing for rest, if any of them were afraid that they would drop down with exhaustion, none expressed their fears. They kept on, urged by their own firm, dogged will power!

Needless to say, the men reached their encampment safely.

Here are a few beautiful lines I read long ago:

It is His will that I should cast
My care on Him each day,
He also bids me not to cast
My confidence away.

But oh! How foolishly I act
When taken unaware,
I cast away my confidence
And carry all my care!

Franklin Roosevelt, who spoke so eloquently about freedom from fear, learnt the hard way how to be free of fear. At the age of thirty-nine, he was struck by a virulent form of polio and was paralysed from the waist down. He was confined to bed for six months and then recovered gradually. But the painful condition stayed with him and he could not walk without support. He was never without pain. He could not dress himself without assistance. He devoted the better part of a decade to a single-minded effort to walk and failed almost completely. His sons had to support him and accompany him from the dais to the podium every time he rose to make a speech, which was quite often. Yet, no American ever thought of him as an invalid. Many of his people actually believed that he had fully recovered from his bout of polio.

I am reminded of Hemingway's immortal words: 'A man may be destroyed, but not defeated.'

We must never underestimate mind-power, the power of the will. Freedom from fear as well as health, happiness and harmony depends on thought-habits. Truly has it been said that even happiness is the product of habitual right-thinking.

Try and imagine a huge slab of ice, one-and-a-half miles square and ninety-two million miles high. It would reach from the earth to the sun.

Scientists tell us that this gigantic cake of ice would be completely melted in thirty seconds, if the full power of the sun was focused upon it.

Mental sunshine is equally powerful! When you have the will to be free of fear, the sunshine of your faith and confidence will melt the ice of insecurity and dread. Mental sunshine will cause the flowers of peace and joy and serenity to bloom wherever you go.

Therefore, cultivate the will to be unafraid, create your own mental sunshine!

There is a beautiful poem by an Elizabethan poet, Sir Edward Dyer, that talks about mind-power:

My mind to me a kingdom is,
Such present joys therein I find,
That it excels all other bliss
That world affords or grows by kind.
Though much I want which most would have
Yet still my mind forbids to crave.

I see how plenty surfeits oft,
And hasty climbers soon do fall;
I see that those which are aloft
Mishap doth threaten most of all;
They get with toil, they keep with fear:
Such cares my mind could never bear.

The poet tells us that the choice is always ours—to become greedy, avaricious, to toil, to become victims of mishap and live with fear—or else decide that our mind 'could never bear' such behaviour. He knows that it is all in the mind. He makes up his mind that he would not fall prey to insecurity, fear and unhappiness.

More often than not, the worst fears come to us not from the outside, but from the mind within. By wielding your will power, by changing your mind, you can change your life! When you sweep the inner kingdom of your mind free of negative feelings, you can eliminate even the fear of death. Sir Edward Dyer put it this way, with beautiful simplicity: 'I loathe not life, nor dread my end.' Ready to face life and tackle it, he was equally unafraid to die.

You can assert your will power to eliminate self-destructive behaviour. You can assert your will to create tranquillity and peace all around you.

There is a wonderful Zen story that tells us about the time of civil war in Korea. A certain general marched his troops through province after province, killing whoever stood in his way, overcoming every obstacle in his path. As his troops advanced to a certain town, people abandoned their homes and fled to the mountains.

When the general arrived, he found the town empty. Nevertheless, he ordered his soldiers to search every nook and corner. Some of them came back to report that there was only one person who remained in the town—a Zen priest, who was seated in a small temple, meditating.

Immediately, the general rushed to the temple. He walked in and found the priest just coming out of his meditation, calm and serene. He pulled out his sword and flashed it before the monk and said, 'Tremble at my sight, you hapless soul! Do you know who I am? I am the one who can run a sword through you without batting an eye!'

Without so much as blinking, the Zen master looked at him and replied calmly, 'And I, Sir, am one who can be run through without batting an eye.'

The general on hearing this bowed and left. He had come face to face with a man who had cultivated the will to be completely free from fear.

3

Never Forget that Fear is a Kind of Atheism

The first *adhyaya* (chapter) of the Gita is entitled *Vishada Yoga*—the section on Arjuna's despondency. *Vishada Yoga* is the beginning of the Gita, and indeed, the first step in spiritual life is *Vishada*, the darkness of the soul. We are overwhelmed by doubts, fears and sorrows—what is the meaning of life? What does it all mean? Why are we here? Where do we go from here?

Even Jesus cried out on the cross: 'My God, my God! Why hast Thou forsaken me?'

Draupadi, too, experienced this darkness of the soul when she cried out, 'Everyone has abandoned me, all have left me—my kinsmen, my brothers, my father, my husbands—even You, O Krishna!'

We have to pass through darkness so that the light can come!

Arjuna is a great warrior, a brave archer. He has come to the battlefield, prepared to fight, confident of victory. He is Drona's greatest pupil, he is Sri Krishna's favourite disciple. But he is confounded by the grave situation that confronts him.

My limbs do fail, my mouth goes dry, my body quivers,
my hair stands on end, my bow slips from my hand,
my skin burns, my mind reels: I am unable to stand.

(Chapter I, slokas 29-30)

Why does the great hero suddenly suffer from nervous fright?

In his weakness, Arjuna fails to listen to the voice within. He quotes teachings from the shastras to Sri Krishna to prove why he should not fight his kinsmen. His mind is under a cloud. He sinks onto his seat and even casts away his bow and arrow! He says he would go into a forest and lead the life of a mendicant.

Arjuna's mental conflict is born out of a fallacy. And Sri Krishna is at hand to lead him out of his despair.

Yield not to unmanliness, O Arjuna!
It does not befit you.
Cast off this impotence of the heart.
Arise, O Arjuna!

(II, 3)

The Lord knows that Arjuna's despair and pity are born of self-delusion—a form of *moha* or attachment. It is a major weakness and must be overcome by the man of true culture and religion. So, to Arjuna is addressed Sri Krishna's appeal for action—*Uttishta! Paramtapa!* The blessed Lord tells Arjuna:

Your words sound wise, indeed, Arjuna!
But you are wasting grief where none is due.
The truly wise in heart never grieve for those who
live, nor yet for those who die!

(II, 11)

We may substitute 'fear' for grief in this context, for often, fear is also a form of delusion.

There is a popular story about a Frenchman, who incurred the displeasure of Napoleon and was put into a dungeon. His friends and family, it seemed, had forsaken him and forgotten his existence. In utter loneliness and despair he took a stone lying in the corner of his cell and carved out the words, NOBODY CARES!

One day, a green shoot came up through the cracks on the damp and moist floor of the dungeon. Gradually, it began to grow and reach out upwards, toward the light in the tiny window at the top of the cell. The prisoner was given just adequate water to drink each day; he saved some of it and poured it on the blade of green, until it grew into a healthy plant with a beautiful blue flower. As the petals of the blue blossom opened, bending its head towards the light, the solitary prisoner crossed out the words previously written on the wall and replaced them with the words: GOD CARES!

There were two friends who, in their youthful arrogance, had rather blatantly proclaimed themselves to be atheists. In old age, one of them fell fatally ill and was tormented by the fear of what lay ahead. The other came to visit him, half afraid that his dying friend would abandon atheism. He took the sick man's hand in his own and said to him, 'Stick to it, friend! Don't give up the belief of a lifetime, just because you are down and out...Stick to it!'

'You fool,' replied the stricken man, 'there is nothing to stick to.'

The Persian poet Saadi put it across boldly: 'I fear God and next to God I fear, most of all, him who fears Him not!'

Robert Ingersoll professed to be an atheist all his life. He heaped ridicule on God, religion, faith and believers. But when he was close to death, his soul was haunted by terror. In his fright, he is actually said to have cried out, 'O God, if there be a God, have mercy on my soul, if I have a soul!'

Caught in the clutches of the Grim Reaper, Death, he seems to have realised that the greatest tragedy of life is to enter Death without God and go into an eternal Godless thereafter!

An atheist French scientist was crossing the Sahara desert with the help of an Arab guide. The Arab was a pious man who believed in God and prayer. Whenever a sandstorm arose in the desert and they were unsure of the way, the Arab would bow down and pray to God for guidance. This annoyed the scientist. 'Who do you think you are talking to?' he asked the Arab contemptuously. 'How do you know there is a God?'

Solemnly, the Arab answered, 'How would you know whether a man passed by your tent at night?'

'Why, by his footprints on the sand!' said the atheist.

'I see God's footprints on the sun, the moon, the stars,' replied the Arab. 'They proclaim His greatness and His power. His presence keeps me from fear!'

There is an amusing piece written anonymously by a writer to prove that even atheists cannot live without God:

'Religion is the opium of the people,' said Karl Marx, the atheist.
'Atheism is an integral part of Marxism,' said Lenin.
'Marxism is materialism. We must combat religion.
This is the ABC of Marxism...Down with
religion, long live atheism,' said Lenin.
'Lenin is God,' said Stalin.

Unfortunately, we are ready to place our faith in wealth, power, strength and intellect. But the giver of all these is God, and if we cannot place our faith in Him, then our own lives are truly lost.

Here is a beautiful prayer attributed to St Teresa:

Let nothing disturb you,
Let nothing frighten you,
All things are passing away;

God never changes.
Patience obtains all things,
Whoever has God lacks nothing;
God alone suffices.

Martin Luther, believed to be the founder of the Protestant Church, had to face a series of difficulties and dangers. One day, his wife found him in a dark mood of depression. She was an intelligent woman who believed in the providence of God. Finding her husband deep in despair, she wore dark clothes and stood before him.

'Why these black clothes?' asked Martin Luther.

The wife quietly answered: 'Don't you know? He is dead!'

'Who is dead?'

'God!'

'How can you say that?' admonished the Christian leader. 'How can God die?'

And the wife said, 'If God is not dead, what reason do you have to be so sad and downcast?'

Martin Luther immediately realised his mistake, put a smile on his face and said, 'Yes, to the devil belongs to be sad!'

There is a touching story told to us concerning Fredrick Douglas, American abolitionist, author and orator. One day, he said in a mournful speech, when things looked dark for his race: 'The white man is against us, governments are against us, the spirit of the times is against us. I see no hope for the coloured race. I am full of sadness and fear.'

Just then a poor old coloured woman rose in the audience and said, 'Fredrick, is God dead?'

Often, many of us behave as though God is dead. I recall how several years ago, something happened which threw me out of gear and I fell into the slough of despondence. I was sad, dejected and depressed.

I met my Beloved Master, Sadhu Vaswani. He looked at my wretched face but once; he did not look again. Nor did he speak to me a single word of comfort. He behaved as if he had not seen me. Living under the same roof, I was denied the privilege of seeing him, whom I loved deeply.

I could not understand what I then took to be Sadhu Vaswani's cold indifference. The old man who resides within everyone, whispered to me: 'Now you know how much he loves you!'

It took me five days to realise that I must be of good cheer before I could be worthy of being admitted in Sadhu Vaswani's presence. Putting on a forced smile, I went up to him and asked for his blessings. He was loving as ever. As he enfolded me in a warm embrace, unbidden tears rolled down my cheeks. He spoke to me affectionately as though nothing had happened. I realised what a blunder I had committed by appearing before him with a sullen face.

Many months later, Sadhu Vaswani spoke to me of St Francis, of the sufferings he had to face. St Francis never renounced the smile on his lips. He was free from melancholy and always looked cheerful. He retained his sunny serenity and his humour. When laying down the rules of discipline, he said to his brothers, 'You shall take care that you do not behave outwardly like melancholy hypocrites. But you shall behave in the Lord, fresh and gay and agreeable!'

The sweet, serene, bright face of St Francis has been one of the inspirations of my life. I have meditated on it, again and again, and on his love-lit eyes. Often, I have recalled to myself one of his wonderful sayings: 'To the devil belongs to be sad, but to us ever to be glad and rejoice in the Lord.' St Francis was an apostle of spiritual cheerfulness. He was never mournful or melancholy, nor ever afraid. In the depths of sorrow, he would suddenly break forth into a song of praise in his beloved master, Jesus.

Of St Francis it is said that one day, he met a disciple whose face wore a look of sadness. Immediately, the saint rebuked him, saying, 'Why this outward grief and sadness? Let it be between you and God. But before me and others, strive to be cheerful. Remember, it is not seemly that a servant of God should show a sad and troubled face before his brethren.'

4

Remember that With God All Things are Possible

Fear freezes the spirit; faith thaws it out, releases it and sets it free—so the wise men tell us. I repeatedly tell my friends that fear is the child of unfaith. Fear and faith cannot exist together.

There are people who argue that faith is an illusory feeling: How can we believe anything unless we see it, they ask.

I would like to give them the words of Thomas Alva Edison: 'We do not know one-millionth part of one per cent about anything,' he writes. 'We don't know what water is. We don't know what light is. We do not know what electricity is; we do not know what gravity is; we do not know anything about magnetism. We have a lot of hypotheses—but that is about all.'

A woman was showing her valuable family heirlooms made of sterling silver to a visiting friend. 'How dreadfully tarnished they seem!' the friend exclaimed. 'I cannot keep them bright unless I use them,' said the woman.

'That is just the way with faith,' the friend replied. 'You cannot keep your faith bright unless you use it!'

When fear knocks at the door of the heart, send your faith to open the door and you will find there is no one there!

The great musician Handel passed through a severely trying time of life. His health was in ruins, his right side completely paralysed. He had lost all his money and his creditors threatened to have him thrown in prison. Handel was so disheartened that he gave into hopelessness and deep despair. The future seemed to be a great big question mark. But with faith in God, he came out of the ordeal and triumphed against all odds. That was when he composed his great piece of music in praise of the Lord—the famous *Hallelujah Chorus* which forms the grand climax of his immortal work, *Messiah*.

Here are a few lines I read from a book called *Travelling Towards Sunrise*:

Can't you still your troubled heart
And make all cares and doubts depart
From out your soul?
You can not.
O faithless man,
Have faith in God—He can!

Have faith in God—He can! If we make this the mantra of our lives, we need never fear anything ever in our lives! Repeat to yourself again and again: *I am not alone. God is with me!* You will find that fear will not touch you.

Fear of death is one of the most dreaded things that can affect people. The best way to overcome fear of death is through faith in God.

A holy man lay on his deathbed. As his end drew near, his devoted disciple began to sob bitterly, saying, 'Master, master, tarry a while longer with us in the land of the living!'

The holy man smiled and said to him, 'I am still in the land of dying but I hope to be soon in the land of the eternal life!'

He continued, 'It matters little whether one lives or dies. If I die I shall be with God and if I live, God will be with me!'

There was a man who was about fifty-six-years old. He had lived a clean and healthy life and had scarcely ever fallen ill. In fact, he would often boast to his friends that he had never even had an injection.

One day, he had an acute attack of indigestion and visited the family doctor for treatment. After a thorough check-up and a battery of tests, the doctor informed him that there was a possibility of a malignant growth in his abdomen for which he would have to undergo surgery.

The man was nearly paralysed with fear.

'How could it be?' he cried in agony. 'You must be mistaken!' he said to the doctor in rising panic. 'I only came to see you about a little indigestion and you say I might have cancer! What will become of me?'

The doctor consoled him as best as he could. But the man was in the grip of a chronic fear as he was admitted in hospital and prepared for emergency surgery on the morrow.

He lay in a cold sweat in his air conditioned room, unable to sleep despite the sedative that had been administered to him.

As he slipped into fitful sleep, he had a strange dream. He stood on the bank of a vast lake. On the shore near him were a row of boats shaped like a rainbow. He got into one of the rainbow boats and started rowing it happily.

He dreamt that when he was halfway across the lake, dark threatening clouds began to appear and a storm arose. The boat rocked wildly as violent waves lashed against it. He grew nervous and panicky.

Just then, in his dream a blaze of light appeared at the opposite end of the boat. It was a beautiful form—a Being of Light as it were. It uttered the following words, 'Why are you afraid? You are not alone—I am with you!'

He woke up from his dream filled with new courage and optimism. He narrated the dream to his family members, who marvelled at its significance.

The next day, as he was wheeled into the operation theatre, he was overcome by another attack of fear and panic and the beautiful dream was quite forgotten!

When he regained consciousness, the surgery had been successfully performed and he was back in his hospital room. His favourite granddaughter stood by his bedside, holding his hand and smiling joyously as he opened his eyes.

'Here is a little card I made for you, Grandpa,' she said, holding out a sketch that she had made. It was a childish drawing of a boat on stormy waters, a man rowing the boat desperately, with words that formed a beautiful rainbow: *You Are Not Alone: I Am With You!*

'This is what is written under the picture of Sri Krishna in our school prayer hall,' the child explained. 'I copied the words because I thought you might like them!'

God speaks to us in several ways to give us hope, courage and faith—if only we are sensitive enough to listen to Him!

There was a young widow who lived with her children in a small apartment in New York. Her husband had passed away a while ago, leaving her to fend for herself and three small children. He had left behind no savings and the family was plunged into poverty. It was the time of the great depression in America and money and work were hard to come by.

The young widow had great faith in the Lord and she had instilled the same faith in her children. She said to them again and again, 'Trust in the Lord! He will never forsake us!'

In order to earn her livelihood and support her children, she had rented a sewing machine, working at night with a dim light, sewing dresses and linen. She kept the home fires burning, as best as she could.

But now, she was up against a wall. One of her customers had gone out of town and her bill was pending. She had to pay for the rental instalment of her sewing machine and the rent collector had warned her that the machine would be taken away if she did not pay the rent within twenty-four hours.

There was a knock at the door. The children trembled in fear. There was not a dime in the flat. What could the mother do? What would become of them if the sewing machine was taken away?

'Mama, Mama, what shall we do?' the children cried in fear.

'Hush my darlings!' the mother comforted them. 'The Lord is with us and we have nothing to fear.'

She rose and opened the door. On the steps stood a stranger with a baby in his arms.

He spoke with urgency. 'Madam, I need your help very badly! You see, my wife has been admitted to hospital with an acute attack of appendicitis. There is no one at home to look after the baby. We have just moved into this neighbourhood and our landlord told us you are the right person to look after our baby while my wife is in hospital. Please accept fifty dollars as an advance from me. Will you please take care of the baby for us?'

The woman stretched out her hands to receive the baby.

'Go in peace, Sir,' she said to the stranger. 'I shall take good care of the baby!'

When the stranger had left, the children crowded round her, laughing happily as the child gurgled and held out his little hand to them.

'Wonderful are the ways of God,' said the woman. 'He never ever forsakes His children!'

Little Tina, all of four-years old, was spending a weekend with her grandmother. They were happily watching television at night when a thunderstorm broke out and the electric supply was cut-off. Their little flat was plunged into darkness.

'I think we should go to bed now,' said the grandmother after some time. 'It's nearly ten o'clock.'

'It's so dark, and I am afraid,' whispered little Tina.

'That's easily set right,' said the grandmother cheerfully, drawing open the curtains of the bedroom window. The child caught a glimpse of the moon in the sky.

'Our lights may be off,' said the old lady. 'But you can see God's light is on!'

'Grandma,' said the child, 'is the moon God's own light?'

'Of course it is!'

The next question was, 'Won't God put out His light and go to sleep?'

'No honey,' smiled the grandmother. 'God never goes to sleep.'

In her simple and beautiful faith, the child said, 'Well, as long as God is awake, I am not afraid!'

A great and wealthy man once said that of all the experiences of his life, he treasured one incident that gave him unmixed joy of the sort he had never ever felt. It happened as he came out of his bank in New York and was about to signal to his chauffeur when a little girl came up to him, looked into his face and put her tiny hand into his great one and said, 'Mister, I am frightened of the traffic. Please take me across the street to the other side.'

'It was a great honour for me to take that trusting child across to the other side,' the man said later. 'It taught me that when I found it difficult to cross hurdles, all I had to do was put my hand in God's hand. He would be as delighted as I was to lead the child across!'

Three students were asked to give their definition of faith. One said, 'Faith is taking hold of God.' The second said, 'Faith is holding on to God.' The third said, 'Faith is not letting go.'

I think each of them was right!

Doubt sees the obstacles
Faith sees the way!
Doubt sees the darkest night,
Faith sees the day!
Doubt dreads to take a step,
Faith soars on high!
Doubt questions, 'Who believes?'
Faith answers, 'I'!

Faith, it is said, sees the invisible, believes the incredible and receives the impossible. Faith is deaf to doubts, dumb to discouragements and blind to impossibilities for it knows nothing but success and optimism. It can lift its hands through threatening clouds and touch Him who can protect you from all harm and danger. Faith, I have heard, can make the uplook good, the outlook bright, the inlook favourable and the future glorious!

A man who was crossing the Atlantic on a steamer asked the captain of the ship why there were two compasses in the steering room.

The captain explained that the 'lower' compass was often affected by the steel in the framework of the ship. 'The pilot steers by the higher compass,' he explained.

That is the way it should be as we steer our ship through the stormy seas of life. The compass of our feelings may be affected by the changing winds of time and circumstances but the higher compass of faith is sure to point us steadily towards God.

A little boy was trapped on the first floor of a burning house. He had climbed onto the ledge of a window to escape the flames and hung precariously on to the windowsill. He was beside himself with terror, clinging on for dear life to the window, unable to look up or down.

A strong neighbour came below the window and shouted to him, 'Drop down Raju and I will catch you!'

On hearing this, the boy just let go and fell safely into the big man's arms. 'I knew you would catch me, Uncle,' he said gratefully, putting his arms around the man's neck.

All we have to do is trust God and we will be free of fear.

A scientist and a holy man were travelling together on a train. The scientist said to the man of God, 'You may not like to hear me say this but I don't think faith can get you anywhere. What really matters is the strength of your personality, the integrity of your character and the sum total of your achievements.'

Just then, the ticket examiner came along and asked to inspect the passengers' tickets. He checked each ticket carefully before he returned it to them and then he passed on.

The holy man said to his travelling companion, 'Did you notice Sir that the ticket examiner looked at the tickets carefully but cast not a glance at us? His concern is with the ticket that entitles us to travel on this train, not with our looks or our achievements. So it is with God. We need faith to win His saving grace. The rest will come with His grace!'

I read the story of two men who were caught in a boat above the rapids of a waterfall. The boat began to swirl dangerously and they were unable to control it. It seemed as if they would be borne away by the rushing waters and dashed to smithereens on the rocks below. In the grip of terror, they screamed for help. People who saw their plight threw a rope at them. One of the men caught the rope firmly. But the other man saw a log floating by the boat and ignoring the rope, laid hold of the log. It proved to be a fatal mistake! While his companion was drawn towards the shore, the man who clung to the loose, floating log was borne irresistibly along and never seen afterwards.

Faith gives us a life-saving connection with God, in whatever circumstances we find ourselves. Faith is always on the shore, holding a rope out to us; when we take hold of it, we are sure to be hauled to safety. And when we have faith in God, we cannot doubt our fellow human beings either. Faith in God will reinforce our faith in fellow human beings and help us understand life and overcome our weaknesses.

Cardinal Manning was passing through a spiritual crisis—a dark period of doubt and despair and loss of faith. He went into a bookshop where he saw one of his own bestselling books, entitled *Faith in God*. He asked for a copy of the same.

As he waited for the book to be brought up from the basement, he heard a clerk calling from downstairs: 'Manning's *Faith in God* all gone!'

The words jolted him out of his despondency and he took them to heart, conquering his depression.

Several years ago, a brave man attempted a near impossible feat across the Niagara Falls. He had a strong wire stretched above the roaring falls and announced that he would walk across the tightrope from the American to the Canadian side.

People were electrified by the news of this death-defying feat and gathered in large numbers on the appointed day to watch the thrilling display. As they held their breath in awe, the man performed the daring stunt with cool, calm deliberation. The crowds cheered wildly!

But the show was not at an end. The performer called for a wheel barrow with grooved wheel and began to push it across the suspended wire. As this breathtaking performance concluded, a thunderous applause broke out on both sides of the Niagara.

A little boy was cheering loudly on the bank as the performer crossed over. The performer asked him, 'Do you believe that I can put you in this wheel barrow and take you across to the other side?'

'I am sure you can, Mister,' said the boy quickly.

'Come along then and get into the wheel barrow,' the man invited. 'Let us show these people how brave you are and how you trust me.'

Without a word, the boy took to his heels, disappearing into the crowd! He had said that he believed in the tightrope walker, but in reality, he had not trusted him enough to accompany him across the falls.

So many of us are like this boy. We say our prayers; we profess faith in the Lord; we call upon Him to pilot us safely across the 'samsara sagar' to the other shore but we fail the test of faith during crucial moments and give in to doubt and despair.

What we need is the kind of faith that will never fail us, the kind of faith that makes us realise that all things are possible to those who believe in His mercy and goodness:

O for a faith that will not shrink
Though pressed by every foe
That will not tremble on the brink
Of any earthly woe!

A faith that shines more bright and clear
When tempests rage without,
That when in danger knows no fear
In darkness feels no doubt.

One of Oliver Cromwell's officers was given to the habit of constant anxiety and worry. His faithful servant was a pious man, who wished to help his worrisome master. The servant said to him, 'Master, is it not true that the Lord ran this world long before you came into it?'

'Sure he did,' assented the master quickly.

'You believe that He will run it after you have left, don't you?' the servant continued.

Again the master nodded assent.

'In that case,' said the servant, 'why don't you stop worrying and let Him run the world while you are in it?'

The servant was a man who knew what it was to live in the present and cast his cares upon the Lord!

Wherever I go, I hear that the world is achieving rapid progress—that more and more people are educated, that many of them are graduates, that per capita income is increasing, people's standard of living is improving, never have we lived so comfortably, so they tell me.

Sadly, is it not also true that we are living in constant stress, tension and insecurity? Aren't we close to spiritual failure? If we are to lead sane, balanced, happy, secure lives, we must re-establish our contact with God.

A friend visited George Muller's orphanage at Bristol and saw first-hand, difficulties that Muller had to contend with just to provide the orphans with food every day. 'How can you live in such permanent insecurity?' he said to Muller. 'You seem to live from hand to mouth!'

'True,' replied Muller. 'It is my mouth, but God's hand!'

5

Learn to Relax in God's Presence so that You Can Receive His Power

I am sure you have often heard spiritual aspirants and teachers talking about practising the presence of God in your life. Have you ever wondered what this phrase means?

Perhaps many people pass through life without ever realising that sense of peace and serenity which is what our elders had in mind when they spoke about practising the presence of God. Unfortunately, the word 'serenity' is something that we only understand in the abstract and not in practice. But serenity is a great gift that can be available to all of us when we are at one with the presence of God.

Imagine your mind to be the surface of a lake. When you are disturbed or agitated, the surface is whipped up by a furious storm. Huge waves arise and lash against the shore in a fury. It seems to be a frightening display of the violent force of wind and water. And then, the wind abates and the waves gradually subside. The lake lies placidly, its surface still and smooth as a mirror.

Our mind, too, is just such a lake. We can calm the spirit when the fury of our thoughts and anxieties are quietened down. It is in such stillness that we achieve strength and peace of mind. It is then that our fears are vanquished and we achieve joy and serenity.

Experts agree that inner calm cannot be achieved by physical exertion. Pacing up and down, clenching our fists and grinding our teeth will not restore calmness to the mind. Instead, we must fill the mind with quiet thoughts that focus on God and His infinite goodness.

The crucial factor here is that state of our awareness, our inner consciousness. We need to realise that we are harnessed to the greatest source of peace, joy, healing and problem-solving. We need to become conscious of our affiliation to God.

God is perfect. God is absolute. God is the source of all that is best in our lives. He is too kind to punish us; He is too wise to make a mistake. All that He sends to us is meant for our own good.

When we are tormented by needless fear, when we are crushed by the blows of fate, we should turn to God in absolute faith and trust. When we link ourselves to Him, we allow positive energies to flow into our lives. Helpful, healing, wholesome thoughts come to us during periods of stillness, prayer and meditation.

I spoke earlier of paying special attention to our inner consciousness. This is especially true of what has been called 'nerve-consciousness'. Fear often leads to extreme nervous tension. When we are nervous, our nerves are overtaxed, leading to severe tension and restlessness. It is only through a relaxed nerve-consciousness that we can feel the healing power of God flowing into us.

Every kind of tension is bad for us, no matter where it originates—through fear, through negative thoughts or through stress. When our nervous system is in disharmony, it is impossible for God's harmonious, healing, health-giving power to bring help and relief to our troubled minds.

When our minds are haunted by fear, the waters of the soul are muddied. We need to retreat so that the soul may be refreshed. And where else can we find such an untroubled retreat as in the quiet depths of our own soul? If the soul is to be cleansed, we need to take a dip in the waters of silence—for silence is a great healer.

Within every one of us is a realm of peace, power and perfection. Through practice, we can, at will, enter this realm and contact God. When we do so, we become conscious of infinite power, a wondrous peace and a beautiful sense of serenity within.

The first step to this inner serenity is relaxation. However, most of the time, we are tense without even realising it. Even when we go to sleep, our body and mind are not relaxed; the fears and tensions of the day persist in our subconscious mind and we fail to enjoy restful sleep. So we wake up the next morning with a feeling of fatigue and mental exhaustion. We do not feel fresh and strong to meet the challenges of the new day. This goes on day after day; the tension and fear keep accumulating until they manifest themselves in one physical illness or the other. So many diseases of the present day—heart attacks, high blood pressure, nervous breakdown, migraine, asthma—are due to this built-up tension. So much so, it is now being said, 'People do not die of diseases; they die of internal combustion.'

We need to relax—relax in the consciousness that we are in God's presence so that His healing power may flow into us.

There are several methods of relaxation and you can follow one that suits you best. Here is a simple, easy, eleven-step method that I recommend:

- Lie on your back on the floor, or sit on the floor in a *sukhasana* (comfortable posture). You may, if you like, sit on a chair with your feet gently touching the floor. Begin by taking a few deep breaths, exhaling very slowly so that the lungs are completely emptied out.
- Imagine yourself in the loving, immediate and personal presence of the Lord. Picture yourself sitting at His Lotus Feet, with your arms girdling His ankles, your head resting at His feet.

Say to yourself: 'Here is true rest. Here is peace. Here is relaxation. In Thy presence, Lord, my fears and frustrations, worries and anxieties, depressions and disappointments, tensions and tribulations vanish as mist before the rising sun. I feel at peace…I am relaxed…'

- At this point, you begin to relax each part of your body, consciously. To relax a muscle, you must first tighten it then let it go. As you let it go, it may perhaps help you to utter the magic words, 'Let go, let go, let God…'
- Turn your attention to the muscles around the eyes. Relax, relax, relax. Open the eyes and imagine that the eyelids have become heavy. Let them drop on the eyes. Lift them and shut them three times.
- Move on to the muscles around the mouth. Tighten them and let go. Relax, relax, relax.
- Relax your facial muscles. Clench your teeth then relax, letting your face go limp. Relax, relax, relax.
- Repeat the process throughout the body: Neck, right shoulder, elbow, forearm, wrist, hand, fingers, left shoulder, elbow, forearm, wrist, hand, fingers, back, chest, abdomen, buttocks, calves, ankles, feet, toes. Push your toes down on the floor, stretch and relax. Pull your feet up towards the legs, stretch and relax. Relax, relax, relax.
- Breathe in deeply; stretch your whole body; relax and exhale. Repeat this three times. Relax, relax, relax. Tell yourself that

you are now relaxed, calm, serene, peaceful. Reinforce the picture of yourself resting joyfully at the Lotus Feet of the Lord—calm, relaxed, serene, peaceful.

- You are now lighter than air, moving upwards, upwards, floating as a cloud—calm, relaxed, peaceful, serene.
- You are in the presence of the Lord. Offer this simple prayer to Him: 'Thou art by me, a living and radiant presence, and I am relaxed, calm, peaceful, serene.'

Repeat this prayer a few times. You are now completely relaxed.

- When you wish to close this exercise in relaxation, rub the palms of your hands together, place them gently on the eyelids and gently open your eyes.

Let me share a moving incident in the life of Gautama Buddha. He learns of the dreaded robber, Angulimala, and goes out alone to meet him. As he passes by the haunt of the robber, he hears a thunderous voice: 'Stand still, O hermit, stand still!'

Angulimala, 'the man with the garland of thumbs' was a fierce bandit who had plundered, looted and killed ruthlessly. His name had been acquired from the horrific practice of chopping off the thumbs of his victims and stringing them as a garland around his neck as a trophy of his bloody deeds.

Now, with a flashing sword in his hand and murder in his heart, the dreaded bandit was chasing the Buddha. He ran as fast as he could but the Buddha eluded him.

Vexed and frustrated, Angulimala cried out from a distance, 'Stand still, O hermit, stand still!'

Quick came the simple, significant answer of the Buddha, 'I am still! May you learn to be still!'

When the bandit confronted him, the Blessed One explained to Angulimala what it was to stand still. The words of the Master went deep into the heart of the robber and he underwent a spiritual conversion. The bandit became a disciple and his heart, in due course, became tranquil as the surface of a lake on a clear, windless day.

To enter into the peace of God is to relax and stand still—wherever you are!

6

Don't Be Afraid of What May Happen Tomorrow!

A woman once lived to be one hundred years of age. When asked the secret of her longevity, she said, 'When I work, I work hard; when I sit, I sit easy; when I worry, I go to sleep!'

If only we would emulate her splendid example, perhaps many of us would live to the ripe old age of a hundred years!

Man is constantly given to worrying about the future. What does this anxiety do for us? It may not empty our tomorrows of sorrow but it will certainly empty our today of its strength. And if the future should bring problems with it, this fear makes you unfit to cope with those problems. Therefore, it has been said, 'Worrying about the future is like a rocking chair. It will keep on moving, but will not get you anywhere!' Such needless fear is like the advance interest you pay on troubles that may never come your way!

I knew of a young couple who were happily married. Their joy knew no bounds when a baby boy was born to them. But the happiness did not last very long. They began to worry about the future of their son. They were fearful that they would not be able to give him the best of everything. They were haunted by the fear of the future.

Eventually, the young man decided that he would leave his wife and child and take up a tough and demanding job in the Middle East.

His logic seemed simple enough. 'Today, people have to pay one lakh rupees for an engineering seat. When my son is eighteen, I shall probably have to pay fifteen lakhs! I must start earning more so that I will be able to pay for his education.'

He did succeed in procuring a highly paid job but conditions were difficult. His family could not live with him or even visit him for he worked on a sensitive military installation. Every year, he was given a fully paid vacation and air tickets to go home and spend time with his family—for just 30 days. As for the rest of the 335 days of the year, his young wife and charming toddler lived alone in their Pune apartment, waiting for his phone calls, longing to see him, and coping with life on their own.

True, they made a lot of money. But they lost their days of joy and warmth and togetherness. He was not at home to see his son crawl, take his first step, cut his first tooth or call out 'Pa-pa' for the first time. He was not there to support his wife when the little one suffered from childhood ailments like measles and wheezing. He was not there to run around for application forms, school interviews and admission procedures when the boy started schooling…

When he was eighteen, the boy had decided on his future career. He successfully applied for admission to the National Defence Academy. He wished to join the Indian Armed Forces and serve his country. And he did not have to pay a paisa for this privilege!

His parents were, of course, happy and proud. But they also felt a little foolish, for their fears for the future had proved to be illusory!

There are many people I know who live in constant fear of what the future holds for them. They anticipate nothing but trouble and fear of the future has become part of their mental make-up. They live in constant insecurity and in doing so, lose much of the joy of living. 'What if the stock exchange crashes?' 'What if I should meet with an accident?' 'What if my child were to fall ill…' And so on and so forth their mind wanders from fear to fear.

I know a few old people who are afraid to go out for a walk or a breath of fresh air. 'If I go out, I may slip and break a bone,' they say, denying themselves one of the simplest and healthiest pleasures of life.

It was Jesus who said, 'Sufficient unto the day is the evil thereof.' God has endowed us with the health and strength that we need. He has blessed us with the means and resources to tackle our life each day, as it comes. He gives us the strength and courage to face each day, each moment of our lives. Why then should we trouble ourselves over the future?

Here's an example of a story that I know plays out in many a household. There was a woman whose daughter was late returning home one night. The time passed, the mother grew frantic with fear. By 9:30 pm, she began calling up the city hospitals to find if a girl had been admitted that evening. She was about to ring the police station when the girl walked into the house, happily humming a tune.

'Where have you been all evening?' screamed the mother.

'Having fun at my friend's surprise birthday party!' laughed the teenager.

And the poor mother had been reduced to a nervous wreck!

I read an old story about an angel who met a man carrying a heavy sack on his back.

'What is it that you carry on your back?' enquired the angel.

'My fears and anxieties and worries,' sighed the man. 'Truly, they are a terrible burden. And try as I might, I just can't get rid of them!'

'Let me take the sack off your back,' said the angel. 'I should like to see those fears and worries of yours.'

When the angel opened the sack, it was found to be empty!

The man was astonished. His fears and anxieties were all about tomorrow—which had not yet arrived!

The angel said to him, 'You have nothing to fear; throw the sack away and walk tall!'

I tell people again and again: You should not make yourself miserable by thinking of the past or of the future. The past is a cancelled cheque. The future is just a promissory note. The present is the only cash in hand—so use it wisely and well. Make the most of the here and the now!

A wealthy man of seventy-five was in a state of extreme anxiety and fear about his future. He could think of nothing except his investments, his gilt-edged bonds, his estate and the interest on his deposits.

'You are better off than most people,' his friends said to him. 'Why do you have to fear for the future?'

'Interest rates are falling,' wailed the old man. 'Real estate prices are not rising any more. Gold is not gaining either. What will happen to my investments? How can I be sure I can maintain my standard of living in my old age?'

It would have been rude to ask the old man what 'old age' he was talking about. He was sure that he was going to live to be a hundred-years old. But he was not sure of gold prices, oil prices, real estate prices, share prices and interest rates! Of what use would it be to tell him that there were a hundred thousand things in the future which none of us can ever anticipate?

There was a working woman who was approached by an insurance agent, promoting a new pension scheme.

'You enjoy a comfortable lifestyle today, Madam,' he said to her earnestly. 'But what will happen to you when you retire? You cannot give up all that you are used to now. And don't forget, you have to allow for inflation too!'

'True,' she agreed, beginning to worry already. 'So, what is your scheme all about?'

'I urge you to invest in our pension scheme, so that you will continue to enjoy the same standard of living even after you retire from work,' the agent told her, pulling out forms and brochures from his briefcase.

'Hmmm…' sighed the lady, her head beginning to spin with the figures and tables he held out before her. 'How much would I have to invest?'

'We can work it out for you very easily, Ma'am,' said the young man enthusiastically, now bringing out his laptop computer. 'We shall feed into our programme your current expenses and anticipated needs and we will get to know exactly how much you must invest so that you can maintain your current standard of living.'

The woman was by now quite intrigued. She watched with fascination as the computer screen flashed question after question at her.

'What is your monthly budget?' was the first question. It was followed by questions on her petrol bill, her food bill, her expenses on clothes and jewels, her preferred holiday destinations, the type of cars she liked to drive, her choice of leisure activities, the state of her health, the average life expectancy in her family and so on.

When all the questions had been answered, the young agent flashed a confident smile and pressed a key. 'In just a moment, Ma'am,' he repeated himself proudly, 'our programme will tell you how much you need to invest in our pension plan so that you can continue to live in the style that you are used to.'

The computer screen blinked and came up with a figure: 1.25 crores. That was the amount the lady would have to save before she retired, in order to 'continue to maintain the standard of living she was used to'!

The poor lady almost fainted with shock. 'I would never earn 1.25 crores in a million years!' she wailed. 'Is this some kind of a joke?'

'Of course not, Ma'am,' the agent assured her solemnly. 'Why, you gave all the inputs yourself! And Ma'am, must allow for inflation twenty years from now…and it is not as bad as you think…to save 1.25 crores in twenty-five years, you only have to save something like three or four lakhs per year!'

'I earn only three or four lakhs a year,' sighed the lady. 'How can I possibly save more than I earn?'

'I must also warn you Ma'am that this holds good for a life expectancy of seventy-five years only. Should you happen to live longer, the figures will have to be revised.'

The lady was left with a headache and a growing sense of fear and insecurity about the future. What should she do? Stop spending money and save it all? Stop buying clothes? Should she plan to live only till sixty? Would there be a drastic fall in her lifestyle when she retired?

Her plight reminds me of a poem I read. It is entitled *When To Worry*, and it goes like this:

When should we worry?
When we see the lilies of the field
Spinning in distress,
Taking thought to manufacture
All their loveliness;
When we see the little birds
Building barns for their store
Then't will be time for us to worry
But not before!

How many of us break our backs to provide against dangers that never come! How many toil to lay up riches which they never enjoy; to provide for exigencies that never happen; to prevent troubles that never come; and they sacrifice present comfort and enjoyment in guarding against the wants of a period they never live to see!

Let us consider the high-powered business executive, jet-setting across the world, expanding his sales, exploring new markets, setting new sales targets and planning expansion and diversification. When he sits down at his desk, he has to draw fully upon his intellectual resources to deal efficiently with the problems before him.

However, many of our executives today are haunted by anxiety and fear. They worry about their next quarter's profit; they are afraid of the competitor's moves; they fear takeover bids; they fear enemies within their camp. And then there are oil prices, export and import hassles, labour problems, manpower shortage and rising taxes. Add to this potent mixture inflation, the growing trouble in Iraq and political uncertainty in South America.

And this is not all! Our executives worry about their jobs, their increments, their promotions and boardroom manoeuvres; they fear for their families and the future of their children. ('Will I be able to afford a foreign education for both my sons?' 'Can I afford to give my daughter the capital she needs to set up her own business?') They worry about the condition of their health and their blood pressure. ('This pain in the chest—is this angina or acidity? Why am I sweating so profusely—is it the air conditioning that is faulty, or is it my tension?')

All the energy and mental effort that should be focused on the job at hand are thus diffused and directed in a hundred different directions. How can they concentrate on problem-solving and success, when their energy is dissipated in mounting fears and anxieties?

That is not all. The sad fact of the matter is that all this fear and anxiety are so pointless and futile. Our executive may sit at his desk and worry all day—but will it improve matters in any way? You know the answer, as well as I do—not at all!

There was a woman saint, who presented a remarkable state of happiness, contentment and peace to those who met her. 'How did you arrive at such a state of peace?' they asked her. 'Pray share with us the secret of your peace and content.'

The saint smiled and said, 'My secret is a very simple one. When I eat, I eat. When I work, I work. When I sleep, I sleep.'

The people were puzzled. They said to her, 'But that is what we do too! We eat when we eat; we work when we work and we sleep when we sleep!'

'No,' she said. 'When you eat, your mind travels far. You think of so many things that you are not even aware of the food you are eating. Your mind is always on other things. You must learn to live in the present!'

Give your best to the present. Concentrate on the task you are doing. Let all your energy and attention be focused on the present moment. When you follow this simple suggestion you will find yourself free from fear and tension.

It is said that J Arthur Rank, the movie magnate, had his own special way of dealing with his fears about the future. He simply decided that every Wednesday would be his worrying day. Whenever any thought of the future or fear for the future entered his mind, he would write it on a piece of paper and put it in a box—then forget all about it. The box would be opened on Wednesday and he would often find that many of his worries and fears had been dissolved by then!

An old lady once remarked to a friend, 'I keep worrying about the future constantly. I can't tell you how afraid I am at times!'

The friend urged her to cast her fears and worries at the Lord's feet and live a life free from fear.

'Oh, but I can't do that!' exclaimed the lady. 'If I don't worry, I begin to feel very bad!'

How sad it is that we should punish ourselves thus! Truly has it been said, 'A day of worry is more exhausting than a day of work.' Honest work seldom hurts us. Nobody has been known to have been killed by hard work. But fear, stress and worry can be fatal.

It was Charles Kingsley who wrote: 'Be not anxious about tomorrow. Do today's duty, fight today's temptations and do not weaken and distract yourself by looking forward to things which are yet to occur. You cannot see them, and you would not understand them if you saw them!'

A French soldier in World War I carried with him this little message as an antidote to fear:

> Of two things, one is certain. Either you are at the front or behind the lines. If you are at the front—of two things, one is certain. Either you are exposed to danger, or you are in a safe place. If you are exposed to danger—of two things, one is certain. Either you are wounded, or you are not wounded. If you are wounded—of two things, one is certain. Either you recover, or you die. If you recover, there is no need to be afraid. If you die, you can't be afraid any more. *So why be afraid?*

There was once a laundry woman who always presented a cheerful, smiling appearance. 'How come you are so happy?' one of her rich customers asked her enviously.

'I'll tell you why I'm so carefree,' she drawled. 'I have no money to lose, so I'm not worried about money. I don't fear for my family because I've handed them over to the Lord and they are His responsibility, not mine. I'm healthy and fit but if I fall sick and die, I'm sure I'm going to heaven! So what is there for me to worry about?'

There is no disputing the fact that worrying about the future does more damage to those who worry rather than the actual things they fear about. And so wise men tell us: Worry does not empty tomorrow of its sorrow; it only empties today of its strength. It has been proven in most cases that over 99 per cent of the things people worry about never actually happen. What a waste of mental and emotional energy!

An ocean liner is built in such a way that the captain can, at the touch of a button, lower massive steel doors that separate watertight compartments in the bulkhead from one another. If the hull of the ship is breached in a disaster, this arrangement can still keep the ship afloat.

In the voyage of our life too, we must learn to bring down the doors that shut out the past with all its errors and failures. Equally, we must also shut out the unborn future so that we may live in the present. When we close the doors that shut out the past and the future, we will find that the ship of life sails smoothly ahead!

'Tomorrow' has become a perennial question mark for some of us. 'What of the morrow?' we keep asking ourselves. 'What about the future?' When tomorrow arrives and becomes today and passes off peacefully, we still fret about the morrows to come.

Would it not be better to leave tomorrow with God? Should we constantly burden our hearts and souls with tomorrow's problems and tomorrow's responsibilities? Can we not walk with God today and trust Him for the morrow?

In his autobiography, Martin Luther tells us that the 'preacher' he loved and admired the most was the little robin in his garden. 'I put crumbs upon my windowsill at night,' Luther writes. 'He hops on to the windowsill whenever he wants his supply and takes only as much as he desires to satisfy his need. Thence he hops to a little tree close by and lifts up his voice to God and sings his carols of praise and gratitude, tucks his little head under his wing and goes fast to sleep—leaving tomorrow to look after itself. He is the best preacher I have on earth!'

How true these words:

To be distressed, look down;
To be distracted, look around;

To be dismayed, look before;
To be delighted, look up;
To be delivered, look to God!

Here is the text I found on a New Year card sent to me:

> *I said to the man at the gate of the year, 'Give me a light so that I may tread safely into the unknown.' He replied, 'Go out into the darkness and put your hand into the hand of God. That shall be to you better than light and safer than a known way.'*

So let me repeat to you: Walk with God today and trust Him for the morrow!

7

Go Out of Your Way to Bring Help and Comfort to Others

The king of Ratnapuri was dying. He had no children and therefore, no successor to his throne. His chancellor, a wise and a learned man, advised the king to choose his successor from among his most faithful followers.

The king summoned Sher Singh and Ramdas—his two devoted knights. Addressing the former first, he said, 'Tell me Sher Singh, if I nominated you as my successor, how would you rule the people?'

'Your Majesty, I shall uphold the power and glory of the sovereign. I shall rule the people with an iron hand and the laws will be imposed with due severity,' said Sher Singh.

Turning to Ramdas, the king said, 'What about you, Ramdas? What kind of king will you be?'

'I shall be a servant of all, your Majesty,' Ramdas replied. 'A true king is one who serves his people. The only difference between him and other servants is that he sits on a throne. And so I shall continue to be to the people what I am to you—a devoted servant.'

Ramdas was chosen to be the king's successor.

Truly has my Beloved Master observed, 'He is truly great who greatly serves.'

Hari was the guard and keeper of a hunting lodge located at the edge of a dense forest. There were rarely any visitors to the lonely place but it was the royal decree that the house should always be well-guarded and well-maintained for the king and his courtiers who often went to hunt in the forest and would use the lodge for a brief rest or even a night's stay.

One day, Hari received a royal decree from the palace. The king would stop by the following day for a meal and a nap. He was to get the best bedchamber ready and prepare a meal fit for the royal visitor.

Hari awoke early the next morning and carried out all the preparations systematically. The king's bedchamber was well-aired and laid with the best linen. A piping hot meal was prepared and kept ready for the king.

Hours passed and by two o'clock in the afternoon, the king had not arrived. Hari stood near the gates of the lodge anxiously, awaiting the arrival of his Royal Master.

At about three o'clock, a battered, bloodstained and badly injured stranger tottered towards the gates of the lodge. Hari rushed out to hold him before he fell. The man had been mauled by a tiger. 'Help me!' he cried to Hari. 'Save me! I am dying!'

Hari led the stranger into the lodge. Hot water was kept ready for the king's bath. Hari used it to bathe and clean the stranger's wounds. He clothed the wounded man in the soft robes that had been laid out for the king. He coaxed the stranger to eat some food, feeding him with the choicest delicacies that had been prepared for the king. When the man had been fed, Hari led him to the king's bedchamber and put the exhausted man to sleep.

Shortly thereafter, the Diwan arrived at the lodge. He had come to inspect the preparations for the king's visit and was incensed to hear Hari's account of the stranger. 'You will answer for this gross misconduct!' he thundered. 'How dare you offer the king's hospitality to a passing beggar? How could you offer him food and drink before His Majesty had eaten? Who do you think is paying your salary? The king shall hear of this and you will be suitably punished...'

'The king has heard of his conduct already,' said the voice from the bedchamber. The Diwan rushed into the room and fell on his knees at the sight of the stranger. 'Your Majesty,' he gasped in amazement, 'How is it that you are here all alone and in this terrible condition?'

The king explained that his hunting party had been attacked by a band of fierce tigers. Some of his men had been killed and others badly wounded. A few had simply taken to their heels, leaving the injured king to fend for himself. He had half-crawled, half-walked his way to the lodge, where the kind-hearted keeper had taken such good care of him. Awakened by the Diwan's angry outburst, he had called out to tell him what had transpired.

'I fell off my horse; I lost my weapons and I appeared before him like a wounded beggar,' said the king. 'He treated me with all the love and compassion that one human being can give to another. He fed me and served me like a king. He was not afraid of punishment or recrimination. He put service before self. He deserves the greatest reward that I can give!'

Love and compassion leave no room for fear!

A few days after the end of World War I, the Prince of Wales went to visit a hospital for the critically injured war veterans. The soldiers being treated at this special centre were so badly wounded and disfigured that they appeared just remnants of their former selves. The Prince moved from one bed to the other with deep emotion. Beside each broken body, he stopped, sat on the bedside stool and chatted for a while. He touched each man with warmth and gratitude, thanking each one for his selfless service to the country. As he completed his rounds, he said to the matron who accompanied him, 'I was told that you had thirty-six hopelessly injured patients here. But I have seen only twenty-nine.'

'It's true, your Majesty,' said the nurse, bowing deeply. 'The others are too badly wounded, in too horrible a condition for you to...' she broke off uncomfortably.

'Too horribly wounded?' said the Prince. 'Is it for their sake that I'm not allowed to visit them?' He looked at the nurse in the eye. 'Or is it for my sake that you do not allow me to see them?'

'For yours, Sir,' said the nurse. 'We feel that you will be deeply disturbed by the sight of those men.'

'In that case, I insist that you must take me to them,' said the Prince.

He was led into a special ward where a few men lay in agony. Some of them had lost their limbs; others had their legs amputated. Here too, the Prince stopped by each bed, thanking the men for their sacrifice.

At the end of the ward was a curtained-off area. As he took a step towards the bed there, the matron stopped him. 'Please do not ask to see that man, your Royal Highness,' she whispered. 'It can be of no good...'

But the Prince persisted and was taken into a darkened alcove where lay a dying soldier—blind, twisted, badly disfigured by exploding mortar.

The Prince went white with shock, his lips were drawn, and tears coursed down his pale cheeks. Impulsively, he bent and kissed the brow of the wounded hero.

The man's eyes flickered open and the ghost of a smile flickered on his lips.

The Prince had what we call 'the human touch'!

I often narrate the story of the boy who asked his mother, 'Mom, why are we here upon this earth?'

'To help others, my son!' replied the mother instantly.

'Fine!' said the son, 'But tell me, why are the others here?'

Very often, we begin to discriminate about whom we should help and who deserves our help more than others.

Long ago, I received a book called *The Greatest Is Love*, in which the story is told of a lawyer who prided himself on being an outstanding scholar on the Law of Moses. He met Jesus and asked to have a discussion on what a man should do to live forever in heaven.

'You are the expert on the subject,' smiled Jesus. 'You tell me, what does Moses' law say about it?'

'It says,' the lawyer replied, clearing his throat peremptorily, 'it says that you must love the Lord with all your heart, all your strength, all your soul and all your mind.'

'Is that all?' asked the Lord.

'Well, it says that you must love your neighbour just as much as you love yourself.'

'Right,' said Jesus. 'So that is all you have to do in order to dwell forever in Heaven.'

Now the lawyer certainly did not love his neighbours as he loved himself. He wanted to argue this point with Jesus—that one could not love all his neighbours.

'Now this is not clear or specific,' he argued. 'For instance, I have so many neighbours. Which of them should I love?'

By way of answer, Jesus narrated to him the parable of the good Samaritan.

A Jew was on his way from Jerusalem to Jericho. He was accosted by a band of robbers who beat him up, stripped him, robbed him of all that he carried with him and left him half-dead by the roadside.

A Jewish priest who passed by the spot a little later, saw the man and hastily crossed over to the other side of the road, averting his eyes. A Jewish temple assistant came along, cast a curious glance at the unconscious form of the man, and walked on.

Then a despised Samaritan came along. He was moved to pity at the sight of the wounded man. He knelt by the man's side, cleaned his wounds and bandaged them. He covered the naked man with a blanket, put him on his donkey and took him to the nearest inn where he nursed him throughout the night.

Next morning, he paid the innkeeper a considerable sum of money to lodge the wounded man and care for him till he came back from his journey. 'I will pay all the money you need,' the Samaritan assured him sincerely.

'Who do you think proved to be a true neighbour for the victim?' the Lord asked the lawyer.

'The one who took pity on him,' murmured the lawyer.

'That is what you must do too,' the Lord said to him.

The Jewish Talmud tells us the story of a man who had three friends—two of them he loved dearly but the other, he did not consider in high esteem.

One day, the man received summons to appear at the king's court of justice. Greatly alarmed by the summons, he anxiously entreated his two best friends to go with him and plead his cause.

The first one flatly refused to accompany him. The second one relented and agreed to accompany him but only as far as the gates of the court and no farther.

Stunned by their refusal, the man reluctantly turned to the friend whom he least admired. To his surprise, this friend not only agreed to go all the way with him but also pleaded his case so effectively before the king that the man was acquitted.

This same Talmudic story has been rewritten as an old English morality play called *Everyman*. Everyman is summoned by Death to appear before God. The 'friend' whom he loves most of all—his worldly wealth—cannot go with him even for a single step of the way. His second 'friend'—his family and his relatives—can only accompany him to the graveside but cannot defend him before the Divine Judge. It is his third friend, whom he does not esteem highly—his Good Deeds—who goes with him right up to the seat of Justice and speaks for him and wins his acquittal!

Wealth does not count; words do not count; actions count! Selfless deeds of kindness and compassion count most of all.

Mr and Mrs Kapoor lived on the top floor of a high-rise building overlooking the sea, in an exclusive suburb of Mumbai. For several years after they moved into their apartment, the other flat on their floor remained vacant. It was said that the owners lived abroad and were not likely to live there.

The Kapoors were very happy with their position. They had exclusive use of the common terrace. They lined the corridors and landing with their potted plants. They enjoyed the terrace and the common areas with the smug satisfaction of the man who said, 'I am monarch of all that I survey'.

Nearly ten years after they came to live there, the neighbours returned. Mr and Mrs Kapoor were not pleased. They peeped through the little watch-hole set on their door and frowned as they heard the din, bustle and laughter of the children and adults as their new neighbours settled in.

Soon thereafter, the doorbell rang. Mr Kapoor, who had been peeping through the watch-hole, tiptoed back into the living room and said to his wife, 'They are here! The lady is carrying a bowl.'

'What a nuisance!' sighed Mrs Kapoor. 'I dare say she has come to borrow sugar or tea or some such thing.'

'Don't encourage that kind of thing!' hissed Mr Kapoor. 'Turn them away immediately. Otherwise, they will start knocking at our door for every little reason.'

'Don't you worry, my dear,' said Mrs Kapoor firmly. 'I shall show the lady her place.'

With her lips firmly pursed and a hostile frown on her brow, she walked up to the door and opened it unsmilingly.

'Good morning!' greeted the couple at the door. The lady held out a crystal dish filled with delicious mithai and dry fruits. 'We are your new neighbours and we have brought you a little prasad after our housewarming puja!'

With a little gesture of friendship, the neighbours had conquered the hostility and selfishness of the Kapoors.

People often quote the saying, 'Charity begins at home', and restrict their help and kindness to their near and dear ones. Yes, indeed, charity may begin at home, but it would indeed be a pity if it stays there! I therefore urge you, in the unforgettable words of my Master, Sadhu Vaswani: Give! Give! Give! Give not only to those you love but also to those who do not love you. Give especially to the unfortunate and the deprived; give to those whom you don't want to give! You will receive much from your giving—you can achieve freedom from fear!

Queen Elizabeth of Hungary often gave alms to the poor. As she handed money and food to them, she would always say, 'I urge you to give alms yourselves!'

'Alas,' they would sigh. 'How can we give when we don't have enough money?'

'All of us cannot open our pocket books, it is true,' the queen would reply, 'but we should never close our hearts. Even if you do not have any money, you do have a heart that can take pity on the needy, eyes to see them, feet to visit them and words to encourage and comfort them!'

True! You can give a smile to everyone you meet. You can give a kind word and kind thoughts to your neighbours. You can give appreciation to your colleagues and friends. You can give hope to the hopeless, encouragement to the timid, happiness to all around you and prayers for the well-being of all humanity.

It is said that a Roman tyrant once troubled a pious and holy man to reveal all his 'treasures' so that they could be confiscated.

The pious man gathered the widows, orphans, the lame, the infirm and the handicapped, who were being fed and cared for by his efforts. 'These,' he said, 'are my treasures. I do not fear to lose them for they are lasting and they cannot be confiscated.'

A kind and compassionate emperor distributed vast quantities of his wealth among the poor in a year of famine.

His brothers said to him, 'Our father and forefathers gathered these treasures over several generations, each adding to those of his father. You are giving away our wealth and theirs! You will surely live to rue this!'

The king said to them: 'My forefathers gathered treasures of money—I have gathered treasures in souls.

'My father gathered treasures for earth—I have gathered treasures for heaven.

'My father gathered treasures for others—I have gathered treasures for myself.'

Truly has it been said, charity is a virtue of the heart, and not the hand.

I know many wealthy men who constantly live in fear of losing their profits. Even their blood pressure seems to rise and fall with the rise and fall of shares in the stock market. They fear taxes; they fear raids; they fear falling interest rates. I would say that it is not just money that makes a man rich. He who gives is richer than he who hoards his wealth. For the hoarder is under psychological pressure, worried about losing what he has. Such a man is poor and impoverished, regardless of how much he has!

When you give, you experience spiritual power, well-being and vitality. When you give, you are alive! You experience an overflowing sense of abundance and joy. This is why giving is so much more joyous than receiving. And as the wise ones of the East and the West have repeatedly emphasised, the greatest gifts that we can give to others are not material things but gifts of ourselves. The greatest gifts are those of love, encouragement, inspiration, kindness, compassion and forgiveness.

Prophet Muhammad said: 'A man's true wealth hereafter is the good he does in this world to his fellow men. When he dies, people will say, "What property he has left behind him?" But the angels will ask, "What good deeds has he sent before him?"'

Therefore, I urge you in the memorable words of Sadhu Vaswani: Give! Give! Give! And you will be abundantly blessed with the peace and joy that passeth—indeed, surpasseth—understanding!